No-Guilt!
CARB DIET
COOK
BOOK

Eat your favorite foods and lose weight

pi

Publications International, Ltd.

Louis Weber, CEO
Publications International, Ltd.
7373 North Cicero Avenue
Lincolnwood, IL 60712

Permission is never granted for commercial purposes.

Contributing Writer: Betsy Hornick, M.S., R.D.

Nutritional Analysis: Linda R. Yoakam, M.S., R.D., L.D.

Pictured on the front cover: *(top to bottom):* Peanut-Sauced Pasta *(page 86),* Whole Grain French Toast *(page 24),* Wilted Spinach Salad with White Beans & Olives *(page 52)* and Chicken, Hummus & Vegetable Wraps *(page 41).*
Pictured on the back cover *(left to right):* Chickpea Burger *(page 132)* and Cherry Parfait Crunch *(page 171).*
Pictured on the inside back cover: Banana Split Breakfast Bowl *(page 22).*

All photographs © Publications International, Ltd. *except* the following:
BrandX: page 5; **©Corbis:** page 18; **PhotoDisc:** pages 14, 19

ISBN-13: 978-1-4508-1524-6
ISBN-10: 1-4508-1524-3

Library of Congress Control Number: 2010939027

Manufactured in U.S.A.

8 7 6 5 4 3 2 1

Nutritional Analysis: Every effort has been made to check the accuracy of the nutritional information that appears with each recipe. However, because numerous variables account for a wide range of values for certain foods, nutritive analyses in this book should be considered approximate. Different results may be obtained by using different nutrient databases and different brand-name products.

Microwave Cooking: Microwave ovens vary in wattage. Use the cooking times as guidelines and check for doneness before adding more time.

Note: This book is for informational purposes and is not intended to provide medical advice. Neither Publications International, Ltd., nor the authors, editors or publisher takes responsibility for any possible consequences from any treatment, procedure, exercise, dietary modification, action, or applications of medication or preparation by any person reading or following the information in this cookbook. The publication of this book does not constitute the practice of medicine, and this cookbook does not replace your physician, pharmacist or health-care specialist. **Before undertaking any course of treatment or nutritional plan, the authors, editors and publisher advise the reader to check with a physician or other health-care provider.**

Publications International, Ltd.

Table of Contents

Count on Carbs for Healthy, Lasting Weight Loss

Carbohydrates are making a comeback. As the quick-fix appeal of low-carb dieting loses its luster, the spotlight is shifting back to the true stars of weight control—fiber-rich carbohydrates. It's a proven fact that nutrient-packed carbs are the foundation of healthy diets throughout the world. And now a growing body of evidence indicates that eating enough satisfying, high-fiber carbs is key not only to losing excess weight but to keeping it off in the long run. That's great news for your taste buds as well as your waistline.

What's There to Love About Carbohydrates?

More than you probably realize! One of the consequences of the low-carb diet fad is that many people feel guilty or fearful about eating carbohydrates, believing that carbs are fattening and therefore bad. But that couldn't be further from the truth. Fiber-filled carbohydrates have the potential to help prevent some of the biggest threats to our well-being, including overweight. For example:

- People with type 2 diabetes who adopt a high-carbohydrate, fiber-rich diet can lower their blood sugar and insulin levels by as much as 10 percent. Fiber helps slow the rate at which the body digests and absorbs carbohydrates in foods, helping to prevent large spikes in blood sugar.

- The fiber naturally found in carbohydrates helps fight heart disease by reducing the amount of cholesterol in the blood.

- Studies show that eating a high-fiber, carbohydrate-centered diet with plenty of fruits, vegetables and whole grains can help ward off certain types of cancer.

- Fiber-rich carbohydrates are a boon to weight control, helping to make you feel full sooner, so you're more likely to eat less. The added bulk also helps you feel full longer.

Still skeptical? Can't shake the guilt that creeps over you when you think of giving in to your body's natural cravings for carbohydrates? Well, consider the following ways that carbs benefit your body and mind.

Carbs power up your body. Carbohydrate is your body's primary source of energy, fueling literally everything you do—moving, breathing, thinking and even digesting your food. And it's the only fuel your brain can use. That's why cutting carbs makes you feel lethargic, fuzzy, irritable and deprived.

Carbs are where the fiber is. Fiber makes you feel full and satisfied after eating. In fact, studies show that people who eat plenty of fiber tend to eat less overall and also tend to weigh less.

Carbs are naturally rich in nutrients. Choosing the right carbs—whole grains, fruits, vegetables, legumes (dried beans and peas), low-fat milk and milk products—helps ensure that your body gets the nutrients it needs for good health and proper functioning, including a wide variety of vitamins, minerals and other beneficial substances.

Carbs help regulate blood sugar levels. Your body converts all the digestible carbohydrates you consume into glucose, or blood sugar, the body's preferred form of fuel. Eating regular meals and snacks that contain a mix of fiber-rich carbs helps to keep the level of glucose in the blood stable, which is especially important for people who have diabetes or are at risk for the disease. But even for healthy folks, maintaining a more stable blood sugar level helps to prevent drastic dips in energy and alertness.

Carbs boost your mood. Eating carbs naturally stimulates the production of serotonin, a body chemical that elevates mood and suppresses appetite. In other words, eating carbs helps you feel good inside and out.

Carbs protect your muscles. When you deprive yourself of carbs and also eat too few calories, your body is forced to break down muscle and convert its protein into energy to fuel your body and brain. Losing muscle slows your metabolism and makes it easier to gain weight.

Weight-Loss Math

How much you weigh depends on the balance you achieve between the number of calories you eat and the number of calories you burn from day to day. Over time, this "energy balance" determines whether you lose, gain or maintain the same weight. Whether you have 5, 15 or 50 pounds to lose, the formula for achieving that weight loss is the same: You need to tip the calorie scale in your favor by regularly taking in fewer calories than you use.

Experts agree that when it comes to controlling your weight, it's calories that count—not the amount of carbohydrate, protein or fat in your diet. On the other hand, because carbohydrate plays such a critical role in keeping you healthy, the experts also strongly recommend that you get a significant portion of your calories from carbohydrate. Fortunately, building your diet around carbohydrate-rich foods such as whole grains, legumes, fruits, vegetables and low-fat milk products makes it easy for you to control your calorie intake in a healthy way, without feeling hungry or depriving your body of valuable nutrients. That's because these foods are nutrient dense: They provide you with a plethora of essential nutrients relative to the calories they contain, plus they pack loads of tummy-filling fiber. In other words, these foods provide more bang for your calorie buck compared to foods that are high in fats and/or sugars but low in useful nutrients.

To lose weight safely, it's also important to drop excess pounds gradually—no more than about a pound a week on average. To lose that weekly pound, you need to consume about 500 fewer calories than you burn on most days. While a deficit of 500 calories may seem like a big hit to your daily calorie balance, it's actually pretty easy to achieve if you select your foods wisely. Counting calories can be tedious, but if you focus on choosing the right carbs in place of less-nutritious and higher-calorie options, make those good carbs a significant part of your diet, and compliment them with lean protein and a moderate amount of healthy fats, then the calories will fall into place. You can help ensure your weight-loss success by adding regular physical activity (an element in the weight-loss equation that we'll discuss later) to your carb-centered diet; the increased activity will raise the number of calories your body burns, making it easier to achieve that 500-calorie deficit.

Carbohydrates and Your Weight

The fear and guilt surrounding carbohydrates probably originated from a misunderstanding of the relationship among carbs, blood sugar and insulin levels. To clear up the confusion, it's important to understand what happens to the carbohydrates you eat.

1. First, the two types of digestible carbohydrates—starches and sugars—are broken down by the body into the smaller sugar units known as glucose.

2. Next, the glucose moves into the blood to be transported to all of the body's cells.

3. Finally, with the help of insulin (a hormone produced by your pancreas), the glucose moves into the body's cells, where it is used as energy to fuel the basic functions of life.

Low-Carb Diets Lose Momentum

Interest in low-carb dieting is declining. It is becoming clear that low-carb diets are:

- Unhealthy—Health experts and leading health organizations, including the American Diabetes Association and the American Heart Association, do not recommend low-carbohydrate diets because of the potential health hazards associated with their high fat content.

- Unrealistic—Following a diet plan that severely restricts basic foods such as breads, cereals, pasta, potatoes, fruits and vegetables is simply not realistic over time. Severely limiting your food choices is a guaranteed way to limit dieting success.

- Unreliable—Studies show that although you can lose weight on a low-carb diet, it is no more effective than other diets, and because it is difficult to stick with, most people regain weight when they resume their usual eating habits.

- Unnatural—The human body is designed to thrive on the energy produced by eating carbohydrates. Depriving your body of the carbs it needs to function at its best can not only make you feel lousy, it can lead to other unpleasant side effects, such as bloating and constipation.

Your body performs best when your blood sugar level is kept relatively steady throughout the day. If your blood sugar drops too low, you become lethargic and feel hungry. If it goes too high, your brain signals your pancreas to secrete more insulin in order to push more glucose into the cells and bring the blood sugar level back down; if there is more glucose in the blood than the cells can take in, however, your body converts that excess energy into fat for storage.

Advocates of low-carb diets claim that eating carbohydrates causes the body to produce excess insulin, which they say leads to insulin resistance, an increased risk for diabetes and weight gain. It is true that when the body's cells grow resistant to insulin, the pancreas must produce more insulin to help transfer glucose from the blood into the body's cells. What is not true is that excess insulin in the body causes weight gain. In reality, experts believe that insulin resistance is the result, not the cause, of being overweight. The combination of eating too many calories—whether from carbohydrate, protein or fat—and living a sedentary lifestyle is the underlying cause of weight gain.

Getting to Know Carbohydrates

Now that you know that carbs aren't the villains they've been made out to be, it's time to get to know them a little better. Carbohydrates include the starches, sugars and fiber in foods. You'll find carbohydrates in many dietary staples, including grain-based foods, fruits, vegetables, legumes and milk products, as well as in foods that have had natural sugars added to them, including nondiet beverages, sweets and desserts. With the exception of fiber (and fiberlike starches), which the body cannot digest, all carbohydrates provide the body with the same amount of energy: four calories per gram. In fact, once digested, your body cannot distinguish between glucose that came from starches and glucose from sugars. The main difference between starches and sugars is the company they keep—in other words, the nutrients that typically accompany these two types of carbohydrate in foods.

Starches, also known as complex carbohydrates, are generally considered the "good carbs." That's because starches are found in grains and grain products, legumes and vegetables—foods that are often rich in fiber, vitamins, minerals and other beneficial nutrients and may help lower the risk of cancer, heart disease and other health problems. Complex carbohydrates that have been refined, such as white flour and white rice, have had most of their fiber removed and are not as nutritious—nor as beneficial for weight control—as their whole grain counterparts, such as whole wheat flour and brown rice.

Sugars, also known as simple carbohydrates, are often thought of as the "bad carbs," again because of the other nutrients they tend to hang around with. Simple carbohydrates include ordinary table sugar, honey and syrup, which are typically most abundant in sweet foods that provide mostly calories and few nutrients. But there are other simple sugars—specifically, the ones found naturally in milk (lactose), fruits (fructose), and some vegetables (sucrose)—that keep good company. The foods that commonly contain these natural sugars also tend to include nutrients that are essential to good health: Milk, for example, contains calcium and other valuable vitamins and minerals, and fruits and vegetables are great sources of various essential vitamins and minerals as well as fiber.

Fiber: A Leading Actor in Weight Loss

When you think about fiber, you probably think "roughage," the stuff that helps to keep you regular. But fiber can have other beneficial and even more important effects on health, including a vital role in weight management. Fiber can be a valuable ally in your efforts to control your weight because it helps you feel full sooner and longer and curbs cravings, making it easier to eat fewer calories. Yet most people get only 12 to 15 grams of fiber each day, which is barely half of the recommended amount.

Fiber falls under the category of carbohydrates, but it is unique because it cannot be digested in the body and therefore does not supply energy the way other carbohydrates do. That's what makes it so good for your health—and your waistline. Not all fibers are alike, however, so it's important to understand the benefits of the different types of fiber. Most foods contain a mixture of two well-known types of fiber—insoluble and soluble. Emerging evidence suggests that a third type of fiber, sometimes called resistant starch (and discussed in the next section), may have some promising, although not proven, health benefits as well.

Insoluble fibers aid in digestion. Insoluble fiber is the roughage in food. It absorbs water like a sponge as it passes through the digestive tract, adding bulk and softness to stools, thus promoting regularity and preventing constipation. Insoluble fibers tend to give food a coarse texture. Foods rich in this type of fiber include wheat bran and bran cereals, nuts and seeds, some vegetables, and the skins of some fruits.

Soluble fibers provide protective benefits. Soluble fiber dissolves as it passes through the digestive tract and becomes a gel-like substance that helps to lower blood cholesterol levels and prevent blood sugar levels from rising too quickly. It also feeds the good bacteria naturally found in the colon and helps support immune function. Food sources of soluble fiber include legumes, oats, barley, nuts, some fruits and vegetables, and psyllium.

Age	Recommended Grams of Fiber Each Day
19–50 years	Men: 38 Women: 25
50+ years	Men: 30 Women: 21

Resistant Starch: A New Frontier in Fiber

Interest in this unique fiber is growing. Although technically a type of starch, this carbohydrate acts like fiber because it "resists" digestion. Resistant starch appears to provide some of the same health benefits of insoluble and soluble fibers—plus some unique advantages of its own. Compared to other types of fiber, resistant starch may have a greater effect on satiety, making you feel full and satisfied longer so you're likely to eat fewer calories overall. Emerging research also suggests that resistant starch may help put your body into a fat-burning mode and reduce the storage of fat. Presently, there are no specific guidelines on how much resistant starch is needed to reap any possible benefits. Resistant starch is not a miracle cure, however, so beware of claims that suggest it is the answer to weight loss. Until more is known, it's wise to focus on eating a variety of unrefined carbs, including those that contain resistant starch. Here's where you'll find this intriguing fiber mimic:

- Resistant starch is present in foods that are naturally rich in fiber, such as whole grains (wheat, oats, barley, brown rice), legumes (beans, lentils), and some fruits and vegetables (bananas, plantains, potatoes, peas, corn).

- Resistant starch forms in some starchy foods once they are cooked and chilled, so you'll find it in the noodles of a cold pasta salad, the chilled rice served with sushi, and the potatoes in traditional cold potato salad.

- Resistant starch can be added to foods— including breads, pasta, cereals, snacks, baked goods, some beverages, mashed potatoes, and casseroles and similar mixed entrées—during manufacturing. In this way, resistant starch helps to boost a food's fiber level and, if used in place of ingredients such as refined flour, helps to lower the food's total calorie load. But you won't see

"resistant starch" listed as an ingredient on the label. Instead, depending on the type of resistant starch added, you may see it listed as cornstarch, resistant cornstarch, maltodextrin or modified food starch.

In Search of Fiber

Fortunately, you don't have to look far to find fiber. And the great thing about fiber is that foods high in fiber are usually low in both calories and fat and packed with important nutrients. The best way to get your fiber is from food rather than supplements, and that's easy if you practice these simple steps:

- Follow the "five-a-day" rule for fruits and vegetables. Get at least five servings of produce (be sure they're not all fruit) each day. Eat fruits and vegetables whole, peeling them only when necessary. And opt for eating the actual produce rather than drinking the juice.

- Go for whole grain breads, cereals, crackers and pasta. Making this simple switch means you don't have to feel guilty about indulging your desire for carbs. It's an easy and enjoyable way to boost the fiber in your diet. Since the words "whole grain" on the label don't guarantee a food is high in fiber, always check the Nutrition Facts panel on the package to be sure the item provides at least 2 or 3 grams of fiber per serving. Compare labels of similar products to find the one that is highest in fiber.

- Get friendly with legumes, such as navy, kidney, pinto and Great Northern beans. These versatile fiber powerhouses can be added to soups, salads, chili and casseroles.

- Look for foods that have been fortified with fiber. Foods that contain added fiber may include breakfast cereals, breads, pasta, yogurt, drink mixes, breakfast and energy bars and even snack foods.

• Boost your fiber intake slowly. If you have not been getting much fiber, add fiber-rich foods to your diet gradually. Adding too much fiber too quickly can cause unpleasant symptoms, such as bloating and gas. Also, be sure to drink plenty of water and other liquids to keep that fiber moving through your system.

Note: A fiber supplement may be appropriate if you're really having trouble getting enough fiber from food. But check with your doctor first, and don't rely on a fiber supplement to take the place of high-fiber foods. It should only help fill your fiber shortfall. Fiber supplements are available as wafers, tablets, and powders. They usually contain 2 to 4 grams of fiber per dose, and most can be taken up to three times per day, adding 6 to 12 grams of fiber to your daily diet.

Fiber Content of Common Foods

High Fiber (> 4 grams)	Medium Fiber (2–4 grams)	Low Fiber (< 2 grams)
Bran cereals, ⅓ to ½ cup	Bran muffin, 1 small	Plain bagel, English muffin, hamburger/hot dog bun, ½ item
Oat bran, 1 cup	Whole wheat bread, 1 slice	White or cracked wheat bread, 1 slice
Barley, cooked, ½ cup	Whole wheat pasta, ½ cup	Cream of wheat, 1 cup
Dried beans, peas, legumes, cooked, ½ cup	Shredded wheat cereal, ½ cup	White rice, cooked, ½ cup
Popcorn, air-popped, 3 cups	Wheat flakes cereal, 1 cup	Soda crackers, 6
Berries (blueberries, strawberries, raspberries), 1 cup	Oatmeal, cooked, 1 cup	Pasta, noodles, ½ cup
Green peas, cooked, ½ cup	Brown rice, cooked, ½ cup	Potato, whipped, no skin, ½ cup
Snow peas, 10 pods	Wheat germ, 1 tablespoon	Applesauce, ½ cup
Baked potato, with skin, 1 medium	Graham crackers, 3	Canned apricots, peaches, ½ cup
Swiss chard, cooked, 1 cup	Whole wheat crackers, 3	Melon, watermelon, 1 cup
Almonds, ¼ cup	Corn, cooked, ½ cup	Most fruit and vegetable juices, ½ to ¾ cup
Fiber-fortified foods	Orange, apple, pear, 1 medium	Asparagus, cooked, 6 spears
	Prunes, raisins, ¼ cup	Cauliflower, raw, ½ cup
	Beans, eggplant, cooked, ½ cup	Cucumbers, mushrooms, zucchini, raw, ½ cup
	Carrots, raw, ½ cup	Romaine lettuce, 1 cup
	Broccoli, brussels sprouts, cooked, ½ cup	Spinach, raw, 1 cup
	Shredded cabbage, 1 cup	Walnuts, ¼ cup
	Peanuts, ¼ cup	
	Peanut butter, 2 tablespoons	
	Sunflower seeds, ¼ cup	

The Glycemic Index: What's the Connection?

The glycemic index (GI) is a system that ranks individual carbohydrate-containing foods by how much each one raises the blood sugar level. The higher a food's GI score, the greater the food's effect on blood sugar. Low-GI foods produce a smaller rise in the blood sugar level. Proponents of a low-GI diet claim that it can help with weight loss and appetite control. Yet, the glycemic index gets mixed reviews from health experts.

How the GI Works

With the exception of fiber (and resistant starch, which acts like fiber), all carbohydrates are broken down into glucose in the body and cause a temporary rise in blood sugar, which is called the glycemic response. In the GI ranking system, carbohydrate-containing foods are assigned an index number from 1 to 100, with 100 being the reference score for glucose, which is pure sugar. (Foods that contain mostly fat and protein do not affect blood sugar levels very much, so their GI scores are not calculated.) A score is assigned to a specific food based on how much a 50-gram portion of that food raises the blood sugar level compared with glucose. Typically, foods are rated high (having a score greater than 70), moderate (56–69) or low (less than 55).

Some starchy foods that have a high GI score may cause high blood sugar levels after meals. High-GI foods include pasta, rice, white bread, potatoes and baked goods. Most nonstarchy vegetables, fruits, legumes and whole grains have a lower GI score. These foods may help prevent high blood sugar after meals. Low-GI foods tend to be less refined and higher in fiber.

What You Should Know About the GI

While choosing foods based on their GI score may seem like a simple strategy to follow in theory, several factors limit the GI's usefulness in practice.

- The GI score of a specific food is not necessarily related to the amount or type of carbohydrate it contains, so relying solely or even mainly on GI scores could lead to some rather unhealthy food choices. For example, potato chips have a lower GI score than a plain baked potato. Carrots and watermelon are high-GI foods, but a chocolate bar has a low GI score.

- The GI score of a single food can vary based on the food's ripeness and variety as well as on storage time, processing and cooking method. For example, the riper a banana becomes, the higher its score rises, yet no matter how ripe a banana is, it still provides the same amount of calories, carbs and nutrients.

- The GI ranking applies to an individual food, but when you eat a combination of foods—as most people do in the real world—the GI ranking is no longer valid. In fact, when you combine a high-GI food such as white bread with meat and cheese, the GI score drops to a more desirable level.

- The glycemic response to a given food will vary based on how much you eat. The glycemic index also doesn't measure how rapidly the blood sugar rises (a rapid spike is more problematic than a gradual increase). Plus, the glycemic response itself can vary widely from person to person.

As you can see, choosing foods by GI score is not necessarily a great way to build a healthful diet that will see you through the long term. Your best bet is still to eat a variety of fiber-rich carbohydrates—including whole grains, legumes, fruits and vegetables—along with moderate portions of lean protein and healthy fats.

And while GI-based diet plans have become popular, there is no evidence to show that following a low-GI diet alone will help people lose weight or control appetite. Diet plans that rely on GI scores as the sole factor in determining which foods are allowed and which are forbidden tend to be low in calories but also limited in food choices and low in overall nutrients. What's more, the net result of following such dictates may not necessarily be a low-GI diet but a diet short on nutrient- and fiber-rich carbohydrates and high in fat, saturated fat and protein.

Carbs: How Much Is Enough—But Not Too Much?

There is an optimal amount of carbohydrate you should eat each day, especially if you are trying to lose weight. It is based on decades of research into how the body uses carbohydrates to function at its best, and it depends on your daily energy needs and how active you are.

It is important to understand that carbohydrate is one of the three main energy-supplying nutrients, along with protein and fat. Both carbohydrate and protein provide four calories per gram, while fat is more than twice as energy dense, providing nine calories for every gram. National health and dietary guidelines recommend that you get your daily calories from a mix of carbohydrate, protein and fat in these proportions:

- Carbohydrate: 45 to 65 percent of daily calories
- Protein: 10 to 35 percent of daily calories
- Fat: 20 to 35 percent of daily calories

If you are fairly active, you'll want carbohydrate to supply more than half of your daily calories. Use the table on the left to estimate your daily calorie needs based on your activity level. Then use the table on the right to see how this translates into the amount of carbohydrate you should be eating each day.

Estimated Daily Energy Needs*

Age	Women	Men
19–20	2,200	2,800
21–25	2,200	2,800
26–30	2,000	2,600
31–35	2,000	2,600
36–40	2,000	2,600
41–45	2,000	2,600
46–50	2,000	2,400
51–55	1,800	2,400
56–60	1,800	2,400
61–65	1,800	2,400
66 and up	1,800	2,200

Daily Calories	Grams of Carbohydrate (50-60% of daily calories)
1,600	200–240
1,800	225–270
2,000	250–300
2,200	275–330
2,400	300–360
2,600	325–390
2,800	350–420
3,000	375–450

Source: Institute of Medicine. *Dietary Reference Intakes for Energy, Carbohydrate, Fiber, Fat, Fatty Acids, Cholesterol, Protein, and Amino Acids.* Washington DC: National Academies Press, 2002.

Based on moderate daily activity of at least 30 minutes up to 60 minutes per day. If you are active for more than 60 minutes per day, add 200 calories; for less than 30 minutes of activity per day, subtract 200 calories.

Let Good Carbs Guide the Way

You may already be getting enough carbohydrate, but chances are you need to improve the quality of the carbohydrate foods you choose if you want to start losing weight and improving your health. This can be as simple as switching to whole grain varieties of bread, pasta, cereals and crackers. And it likely means working in more legumes and substituting a variety of fruits and vegetables for most of the less-nutritious, higher-calorie carbohydrate foods you typically consume. The good news is that when you choose higher-quality carbs, you'll automatically get more fiber and likely consume fewer calories overall. Here are a few simple rules to help you build a diet that's well-balanced, providing the optimal amounts of carbohydrate and fiber along with lean protein and healthy fats.

Eat more fiber-rich carbohydrates, such as whole grains, vegetables, fruits and legumes. To do so:

- **Fill up on fruits and vegetables.** Most adults should aim for nine daily servings of fruits and vegetables. It may sound like a lot, but it translates into 2 cups of fruit and 2½ cups of vegetables. Fruits and vegetables are not only low in calories but high in water and fiber, which help to suppress hunger and increase fullness. If you fill roughly half your plate with fruits and vegetables at every meal, you'll have no trouble reaching this goal.

- **Make half your grains whole.** To get the most from your grain choices, make at least three of your servings whole grain, such as whole wheat bread, brown rice, oatmeal, barley or whole grain cereal. To find a whole grain food, look to see if a whole grain, such as whole wheat or whole oats, is listed as the first ingredient.

- **Get to know legumes.** If you've never been a fan of beans and peas, it's about time you become a convert. There are so many options—kidney beans, black beans, cannellini beans, pinto beans, chickpeas and split peas, to name just a few—you're sure to find some that tempt your taste buds. Canned varieties are convenient to use, store well, and are great for adding color, texture and loads of fiber to all sorts of dishes, including pastas, soups, stews and salads. You can also mash them and add them to burgers, meat loaf, and even brownies and cookies to boost the fiber and nutrient content of these foods.

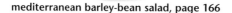

mediterranean barley-bean salad, page 166

Get enough low-fat and fat-free milk and milk products, lean meats, poultry, fish, eggs and nuts. These foods supply protein along with other essential nutrients, including heart-healthy omega-3 fats (found in fish) and monounsaturated fats (in nuts). To get a healthy share of the right kinds of protein foods and good-for-you fats:

- **Follow the three-a-day dairy rule.** Everyone over nine years of age should get three daily servings of dairy—milk, yogurt and/or cheese—preferably low-fat or nonfat varieties. In addition to providing calcium for strong bones, dairy foods supply lactose, a natural sugar, along with several key nutrients that many people fall short on, including vitamin D, potassium, magnesium and vitamin A. Some of these nutrients may also help lower or even prevent high blood pressure.

- **Go lean with protein.** Protein can help you maintain muscle and lose body fat when you're following a reduced-calorie diet that includes regular exercise. Some protein foods provide higher amounts of fat, especially saturated fat, which can increase your risk for heart disease. The key is choosing leaner and lower-fat protein foods. Start with lean cuts of meat and trim fat before cooking, avoid eating poultry skin, and use low-fat cooking methods such as broiling, baking or grilling for meats.

Eat fewer high-energy, low-nutrient carbohydrates, such as sugary snacks, pastries, sugar-sweetened soft drinks, candy, cookies and chips. Most processed, packaged snack foods fall into this category as well. These foods provide plenty of calories but little or no nutritional value; that's why we say they're full of "empty calories." Some of these foods also contain saturated and trans fats that are bad for your heart.

fruited granola, page 34

Carb-Advantage Snacking

When you snack, snack with a purpose—to obtain nutrients needed for good health and to help keep hunger at bay until your next meal. Use carbohydrates to your advantage in snacking by pairing them with other foods so your snack represents at least two food groups. For example, combine fiber-rich carbs with a protein food for the most satisfaction. Here are just a few ideas to get you started:

- String cheese and fresh fruit
- Apple slices and peanut butter
- Whole grain crackers or baked chips with hummus or cheese
- Trail mix (make your own with whole grain cereal, pretzels, dried fruit and nuts)
- Mini sandwich on a dinner roll
- Whole grain cereal and low-fat milk
- Raw veggies with low-fat cottage cheese
- Granola bar and low-fat yogurt
- Mini whole grain waffle with peanut butter or cream cheese

Tips for Tracking Your Carbohydrates

It isn't necessary to track your carbohydrate grams every day, but doing so for even a few days will help you gain valuable insight into how to build a healthier diet that includes the right amount of quality carbohydrates. The recipes in this book list the amount of carbohydrates per serving. For packaged foods, you'll find the "Total Carbohydrate" amount on the product's Nutrition Facts label. Remember, too, to count the fiber in grains, fruits and vegetables. Use this chart to find the approximate amount of carbohydrate in general categories of foods:

Food	Serving Size	Carbohydrates (grams per serving)
Cereals; grains; pasta; breads; crackers; snacks; starchy vegetables (corn, peas, potatoes, winter squash); and cooked beans, peas and lentils	• ½ cup cooked cereal, grain or starchy vegetable • ⅓ cup cooked rice or pasta • 1 ounce bread product, such as 1 slice bread or ½ bagel • ¾ to 1 ounce most crackers and snack foods	15
Unsweetened fresh, frozen, canned or dried fruits and fruit juices	• ½ cup canned or unsweetened fruit juice • ¾ to 1 cup berries or chopped fresh fruit • 1 small fresh fruit (about 4 ounces) • 2 tablespoons dried fruit	15
Milk (all varieties), yogurt and nondairy foods (rice drink, soy milk)	• 1 cup milk or milk substitute drink • 1 cup yogurt, plain or flavored with an artificial sweetener • ½ cup fruit-flavored yogurt	12
Nonstarchy vegetables (e.g. asparagus, broccoli, cucumber, green beans, carrots, cabbage, celery, mushrooms, onions, tomatoes)	• ½ cup cooked vegetables or vegetable juice • 1 cup raw vegetables	5

Understanding Sugars on the Label

The amount of "Sugars" per serving is included in the "Total Carbohydrates" figure on the Nutrition Facts label. But keep in mind that this number includes both the sugars that are naturally present in fruit, milk and some vegetables as well as any added sugars. Unfortunately, there is no way to know exactly how much sugar is added to a packaged food. That's why you'll want to scan the ingredients list of a food or drink to find the added sugar.

On food labels, all ingredients are listed in descending order by weight. The relative position of sugar in a list of ingredients can give you an idea of whether the food contains a lot of sugar or just a bit. Added sugars go by many different names, but they are all sources of extra calories and few or no nutrients. And your body doesn't need to get any carbohydrate from added sugar. A good rule of thumb is to skip products that have added sugar at or near the top of the ingredient list or that have several sources of added sugar sprinkled throughout the list.

Here are a few of the names for added sugar that you may see on food labels:

- Agave nectar
- Brown sugar
- Cane crystals
- Cane sugar
- Corn sweetener
- Corn syrup
- Crystalline fructose
- Dextrose
- Evaporated cane juice
- Fructose
- Fruit juice concentrates
- Glucose
- High-fructose corn syrup
- Honey
- Invert sugar
- Lactose
- Maltose
- Malt syrup
- Molasses
- Raw sugar
- Sucrose
- Sugar
- Syrup

Snapshot of a Healthy, Carbohydrate-Rich Diet

With the help of the recipes in this book, you can build a healthy diet that includes the right amount of nutritious carbohydrates to help fuel your body while you lose weight. The following is simply an example of the types of healthy, carbohydrate-containing foods you could enjoy in one day on an 1,800-calorie-per-day diet that gets about half its calories from carbs (226 grams of carbs, to be specific, which provide about 904 calories). Carbohydrates are just one piece of the puzzle, of course, so be sure to check out "Putting It All Together" on page 16 to see how all of the food groups fit into a healthy, balanced diet.

Grams of carbohydrate

Whole grain cereal (1 cup) with milk (1 cup)	27
Sliced strawberries (½ cup)	15
English muffin (½ muffin) with margarine	15
Sandwich (2 slices of whole wheat bread)	30
Baby carrots (12)	5
Banana (1 small)	15
Yogurt (¾ cup)	12
Spaghetti with sauce (1 cup whole grain pasta)	45
Garlic bread (1 slice)	15
Garden salad (1 cup)	5
Low-fat milk (1 cup)	12
Chocolate chip cookie	15
Popcorn (3 cups)	15

Total carbohydrate = 226 grams

santa fe rotini, page 102

Putting It All Together

Here is a snapshot of how the daily nutrient goals could be met for three different calorie levels.

Food Group	1,600 Calories	2,000 Calories	2,400 Calories	Size Guidelines
Fruits	3 servings (1½ cups)	4 servings (2 cups)	4 servings (2 cups)	½ cup serving: • ½ cup fresh, frozen or canned fruit • 1 medium fruit • ½ cup dried fruit • ½ cup fruit juice
Vegetables	4 servings (2 cups)	5 servings 2½ cups)	6 servings (3 cups)	½ cup serving: • ½ cup cut-up raw or cooked vegetables • 1 cup raw leafy vegetables • ½ cup vegetable juice
Grains (at least 3 servings of whole grain)	5 servings (5 ounces)	6 servings (6 ounces)	8 servings (8 ounces)	1 ounce serving: • 1 slice bread • 1 cup dry cereal • ½ cup cooked rice, pasta or cereal
Lean meat and beans	5 ounces	5½ ounces	6½ ounces	1 ounce serving: • 1 ounce cooked lean meat, poultry or fish • 1 egg • ½ cup cooked dried beans or tofu • 1 tablespoon peanut butter • ½ ounce nuts or seeds
Milk	3 cups	3 cups	3 cups	1 cup serving: • 1 cup low-fat or fat-free milk or yogurt • 1½ ounces low-fat or fat-free natural cheese • 2 ounces low-fat or fat-free processed cheese
Oils* (includes soft margarine with zero trans fat)	5 teaspoons (22g)	6 teaspoons (27g)	7 teaspoons (31g)	1 teaspoon serving: • 1 teaspoon vegetable oil or soft margarine • 2 tablespoons light salad dressing • 1 tablespoon low-fat mayonnaise

Amounts added to foods during processing or cooking or at the table.

Stocking a Carb-Friendly Kitchen

When you have the right carbs on hand, creating a healthy meal or snack can be a snap. Try to keep your kitchen cupboard and freezer stocked with recipe basics; that way, you'll just need to fill in with perishables for each week's recipes. Here's a smart-carb stocking list to get you started:

Grains
- Healthy grain staples such as instant brown rice, whole wheat pasta, barley, quinoa and wild rice
- Whole wheat bread, buns and tortillas for healthy sandwiches and wraps
- Whole grain cereals, including oatmeal, that provide at least 3 grams of fiber per serving
- Baked tortilla chips, baked potato chips, and multigrain chips, pretzels and crackers
- Legumes such as lentils, black beans, chickpeas, black-eyed peas, navy beans, kidney beans and lima beans. Canned beans are a quick and convenient option.

Fruits and Vegetables
- Recipe and soup starters such as garlic, onions, carrots and celery
- Canned tomatoes—diced, stewed, sauce and paste
- Potatoes—white, red, sweet or Yukon Gold. Frozen hash brown potatoes, diced potatoes or baked French fries are easy to keep on hand.
- Frozen corn, peas and other vegetables to add to recipes or for a quick vegetable side dish
- Fresh fruits such as bananas, apples, pears, grapes and avocados
- Frozen fruit and berries to make smoothies or frozen desserts
- Leafy greens such as spinach, kale or Swiss chard for adding to soups, casseroles, chili, egg dishes and meat loaf
- Dark green lettuce for salads, plus salad add-ins such as dried fruit, nuts, beans and seeds

Milk Products
- Low-fat or fat-free milk and yogurt
- Reduced fat cheese—sliced and shredded varieties. Experiment with strong cheeses, such as aged Parmesan or blue cheese: A small amount can add intense flavor along with nutrients to salads, pasta and soups.

Other
- Healthy fats and oils, such as olive oil and canola oil, for cooking. You can also try specialty oils such as peanut, sesame or truffle oil to add flavor.
- Unsalted nuts, such as almonds, walnuts, cashews, peanuts and pistachios, for snacking and recipes
- Vinegars, such as balsamic, red wine and rice vinegar, for salads and veggies
- Broth, such as chicken, beef or vegetable, in lower-fat, lower-sodium versions if possible

Strategies for Success

To look and feel your best, follow these tips for making sure your diet is balanced, nutritious, delicious, and, perhaps most importantly, realistic. What's important is to find a style of eating that is more than a short-term fix; it needs to be one you can live with—and enjoy!—for the long haul.

Eat regular meals. Skipping meals is a surefire way to sabotage your diet when you're trying to lose weight. Extreme hunger makes it more likely that you will overeat at your next meal. Always start your day with breakfast, even if you don't feel hungry. Keep healthy snacks with you at all times so you're not tempted by vending machines or the fast-food drive-thru.

Eat—don't drink—your carbs. Liquid calories can add up quickly, even from healthy beverages like 100 percent fruit juice. Go easy on juice and other caloric beverages (soft drinks, juice drinks, sports drinks) and instead drink water (perhaps flavored with a twist of lemon or lime) and other noncaloric beverages. Whole foods, especially fiber-rich carbohydrates, are more satisfying and help keep you feeling full longer.

Enjoy your favorites—in reasonable amounts. Eliminating foods from your diet or making any food taboo may actually make it harder for you to reach your diet and health goals. When you take a positive approach to eating, you can allow yourself to enjoy sensible amounts of all foods, including favorite foods that might not be the healthiest. The key is to enjoy these foods only occasionally and in small amounts. When you know you'll be around foods that might tempt you to overindulge, make it a point to eat a healthy meal or snack in advance so you're not ravenous and will be able to stop after a taste. If you didn't have a chance to prepare yourself ahead of time, try tricking your stomach into feeling full by drinking a couple glasses of water before facing temptation.

Slim down your portions. Even the healthiest foods can tip the calorie scales if you overdo your portions. Make a conscious effort to pay attention to your portions. Use some simple tactics to prevent oversized portions: Try putting your food on your plate away from the table (so you're not tempted to keep adding more food to your plate), use a smaller plate, sit down to eat your meal, and never eat directly out of a package (put even your snacks on a plate, then close the package and sit down to eat them). Use the visual clues that follow to estimate the size of your portions and compare them to the recommended serving sizes in "Putting It All Together" on page 16. And remember that it's okay to eat a larger portion at a meal or snack on occasion; just aim to stay within the guidelines for daily intake by adjusting the size and/or content of your other meals and snacks that day.

- 1 cup = a baseball
- 1 medium piece of fruit = a tennis ball
- 3 ounces meat, poultry or fish = a deck of cards
- 1 medium potato or ½ cup beans, rice or pasta = a computer mouse
- 1 ounce nuts = a woman's handful
- 1½ ounces hard cheese = a 9-volt battery

Don't forget to partner your eating with physical activity. Food and physical activity need to go hand in hand. Regular activity not only burns calories, it can help to suppress your appetite. Plus, research has shown that getting regular exercise provides people with extra motivation to make better food choices.

Slow down and enjoy. Be mindful as you eat. That means you should sit down and pay attention to the flavors, aromas and textures of the foods you're eating rather than allowing a television, computer, cell phone or newspaper to distract your focus during a meal or snack. Eat slowly and with purpose, and you'll find you're better able to tune into the signals your body sends to tell you it's hungry or full.

Choosing a Safe and Effective Weight-Loss Plan

If you feel you need a more structured weight-loss plan, look for one that follows these guidelines:

- Does not advocate taking in fewer than 1,200 calories each day
- Recommends losing no more than two pounds per week
- Includes regular physical activity
- Includes foods from all the major food groups
- Does not make any foods forbidden
- Does not require special foods or supplements
- Encourages lifelong, healthful eating habits
- Allows the diet to be individualized to fit your lifestyle

On Your "Weigh" to Being More Active

An important part of losing weight—and keeping it off—is spending time being physically active. The 2008 Physical Activity Guidelines for Americans provide science-based guidelines on the types and amounts of physical activity that offer substantial health benefits to Americans ages six and older. These recommendations include:

- The weekly target amount of physical activity (at least 150 minutes—or 2½ hours—spent being active) can be accumulated in spurts throughout the week rather than on a daily basis.

- Exercise that's moderate or vigorous in intensity, or a combination of both, can be counted toward reaching physical activity goals.

- Muscle-strengthening activities are recommended on two or more days per week and should work all major muscle groups (legs, hips, back, abdomen, chest, shoulders and arms).

Remember: Any type of physical activity you do will increase the number of calories your body uses. So think of ways to make physical activity a regular part of your lifestyle. You can schedule structured activities, such as exercise classes or tennis lessons, into your day if that's more likely to get and keep you moving. Or you can focus on adding short segments of moderate-intensity physical activity throughout your day. This approach can include activities you already do, as long as you skip the "energy-saving" devices and strategies as much as possible. For example, use a push mower to cut the grass, wash the car or the dishes by hand, or divide the laundry into smaller batches that you carry up the stairs in multiple trips. Other examples of moderate-intensity activity include walking briskly (which you can do while running errands or going to a house of worship, for instance), raking leaves, dancing and jumping rope. Basically any continuous activity that uses the large muscles in your arms and legs and gets your heart pumping will work.

There are lots of ways to burn calories—and the more you do, the more you'll burn, and the more likely you will be to lose weight and keep it off. (See the box below for additional easy ways to burn calories.) If you haven't been active recently, start slowly and increase your pace and duration gradually. And be sure to check with your doctor before you add any vigorous activity, especially if you have any chronic health problems, such as heart disease, hypertension, osteoporosis or diabetes. Then get moving toward your weight-loss goals!

10 Easy Ways to Burn 100 Calories

- Steady cycling for 10 minutes
- Working out to a fitness video for 10 to 15 minutes
- Brisk walking for 15 minutes
- Climbing stairs for 15 to 20 minutes
- Doing housework for 20 minutes
- Gardening for 25 to 30 minutes
- Washing and waxing the car for 20 to 30 minutes
- Dancing for 20 minutes
- Grocery shopping for 30 to 40 minutes
- Pushing a lawn mower for 15 to 20 minutes

breakfast & brunch

sweet potato & turkey sausage hash

1 link (4 ounces) mild or hot turkey Italian sausage
1 small red onion, finely chopped
1 small red bell pepper, finely chopped
1 small sweet potato, peeled and cut into ½-inch cubes
¼ teaspoon salt (optional)
¼ teaspoon black pepper
⅛ teaspoon cumin
⅛ teaspoon red pepper flakes

1. Remove sausage from casing; shape into ½-inch balls. Spray large nonstick skillet with nonstick cooking spray.

2. Add sausage to skillet; cook over medium heat 3 to 5 minutes or until browned, stirring frequently. Remove sausage and set aside.

3. Spray skillet again. Add onion, bell pepper, sweet potato, salt, if desired, black pepper, cumin and red pepper flakes; cook and stir 5 to 8 minutes or until sweet potato is almost tender.

4. Stir sausage back into skillet; cook 5 minutes without stirring or until hash is lightly browned on bottom. *Makes 2 servings*

Nutrients per Serving

Calories: 186, **Total Fat:** 4g, **Saturated Fat:** 1g, **Cholesterol:** 17mg, **Sodium:** 417mg, **Carbohydrate:** 23g, **Fiber:** 4g, **Protein:** 13g

banana split breakfast bowl

2½ tablespoons sliced almonds
2½ tablespoons chopped walnuts
  3 cups vanilla fat-free yogurt
1⅓ cups sliced strawberries (about 12 medium)
  2 bananas, sliced
  ½ cup drained pineapple tidbits

1. Spread almonds and walnuts in single layer in small heavy skillet. Cook and stir over medium heat 1 to 2 minutes or until nuts are lightly browned. Immediately remove from skillet; cool before using.

2. Spread yogurt in medium bowl. Layer strawberries, banana slices and pineapple tidbits over yogurt. Sprinkle with almonds and walnuts.　　*Makes 4 servings*

Note: This recipe can be also made with frozen strawberries or frozen bananas.

Nutrients per Serving

Calories: 268, **Total Fat:** 5g, **Saturated Fat:** <1g, **Cholesterol:** 0mg, **Sodium:** 112mg, **Carbohydrate:** 50g, **Fiber:** 5g, **Protein:** 10g

slow cooker apple cinnamon oatmeal

1½ cups steel-cut or old-fashioned oats
  3 cups water
  2 cups chopped peeled apples
  ¼ cup sliced almonds
  ½ teaspoon ground cinnamon

Slow Cooker Directions

Combine oats, water, apples, almonds and cinnamon in slow cooker. Cover; cook on LOW 8 hours.　　*Makes 6 servings*

Nutrients per Serving (about ½ cup)

Calories: 119, **Total Fat:** 3g, **Saturated Fat:** <1g, **Cholesterol:** 0mg, **Sodium:** <1mg, **Carbohydrate:** 20g, **Fiber:** 4g, **Protein:** 3g

whole grain french toast

½ cup egg substitute *or* 2 egg whites
¼ cup low-fat (1%) milk
½ teaspoon ground cinnamon
¼ teaspoon ground nutmeg
 4 teaspoons butter
 8 slices 100% whole wheat bread or multigrain bread
⅓ cup pure maple syrup
 1 cup fresh blueberries
 2 teaspoons powdered sugar

1. Heat oven to 400°F. Spray baking sheet with nonstick cooking spray.

2. Whisk egg substitute, milk, cinnamon and nutmeg in shallow dish or pie plate until well blended.

3. Melt 1 teaspoon butter in large nonstick skillet over medium heat. Quickly dip each bread slice in milk mixture to lightly coat both sides; let excess mixture drip back onto plate. Cook 2 slices at a time in skillet about 2 minutes per side or until golden brown. Transfer French toast to baking sheet. Repeat with remaining butter, bread and milk mixture. Bake 5 to 6 minutes or until heated through.

4. Pour syrup in small microwavable bowl. Microwave on HIGH 30 seconds or until bubbly. Stir in blueberries. Transfer French toast to four serving plates; top evenly with blueberry mixture and sprinkle with powdered sugar.   *Makes 4 servings*

Nutrients per Serving (2 slices French toast with ¼ cup blueberry mixture)

Calories: 251, **Total Fat:** 6g, **Saturated Fat:** 3g, **Cholesterol:** 11mg, **Sodium:** 324mg, **Carbohydrate:** 46g, **Fiber:** 5g, **Protein:** 12g

ham & egg breakfast panini

¼ cup chopped green or red bell pepper

2 tablespoons sliced green onion

1 slice (1 ounce) reduced-fat smoked deli ham, chopped (¼ cup)

½ cup cholesterol-free egg substitute

  Black pepper

4 slices multigrain or whole grain bread

2 slices (¾ ounces each) reduced-fat Cheddar or Swiss cheese

1. Spray small skillet with nonstick cooking spray; heat over medium heat. Add bell pepper and green onion; cook and stir 4 minutes or until vegetables begin to soften. Stir in ham.

2. Combine egg substitute and black pepper in small bowl; pour into skillet. Cook about 2 minutes, stirring occasionally, until egg mixture is almost set.

3. Heat grill pan or medium skillet over medium heat. Spray one side of each bread slice with cooking spray; turn bread over. Top each of 2 bread slices with 1 slice cheese and half of egg mixture. Top with remaining bread slices.

4. Grill sandwiches about 2 minutes per side, pressing lightly with spatula, until toasted. (If desired, cover pan with lid during last 2 minutes of cooking to melt cheese.) Cut sandwiches in half; serve immediately.   *Makes 2 sandwiches*

Nutrients per Serving (1 sandwich)

Calories: 271, **Total Fat:** 5g, **Saturated Fat:** 1g, **Cholesterol:** 9mg, **Sodium:** 577mg, **Carbohydrate:** 30g, **Fiber:** 6g, **Protein:** 24g

cherry-orange oatmeal

1 can (11 ounces) mandarin orange segments in light syrup, drained and rinsed

1 cup fresh pitted cherries or frozen dark sweet cherries

2 cups water

1 cup old-fashioned oats

2 tablespoons sucralose-based sugar substitute or granulated sugar

1 tablespoon unsweetened cocoa powder

1. Set aside 8 orange segments and 4 cherries for garnish. Combine water, remaining orange segments, remaining cherries, oats, sugar substitute and cocoa in medium microwavable bowl. Microwave on HIGH 2 minutes. Stir; microwave 4 minutes.

2. Divide mixture evenly between four serving bowls. Garnish with reserved oranges and cherries.   *Makes 4 servings*

Nutrients per Serving (¾ cup)

Calories: 150, **Total Fat:** 2g, **Saturated Fat:** <1g, **Cholesterol:** 0mg, **Sodium:** 6mg, **Carbohydrate:** 39g, **Fiber:** 3g, **Protein:** 4g

breakfast pom smoothie

1 small ripe banana

½ cup mixed berries

¾ cup pomegranate juice

⅓ to ½ cup soymilk or milk

Blend banana and berries in blender or food processor until smooth. Add juice and soymilk; blend until smooth.   *Makes 1 serving*

Variations: Substitute pomegranate-blueberry juice for the pomegranate juice. Add 2 tablespoons plain yogurt, or substitute yogurt for the soymilk. Substitute strawberries, blueberries, raspberries or blackberries for the mixed berries.

Nutrients per Serving (12 ounces)

Calories: 253, **Total Fat:** 1g, **Saturated Fat:** <1g, **Cholesterol:** 0mg, **Sodium:** 35mg, **Carbohydrate:** 59g, **Fiber:** 6g, **Protein:** 3g

mixed berry whole grain coffee cake

1¼ cups all-purpose flour, divided
¾ cup quick oats
¾ cup packed light brown sugar
3 tablespoons butter, softened
1 cup whole wheat flour
1 cup fat-free (skim) milk
¾ cup granulated sugar
¼ cup canola oil
1 egg, slightly beaten
1 tablespoon baking powder
1 teaspoon ground cinnamon
½ teaspoon salt
1½ cups frozen unsweetened mixed berries, thawed and drained *or*
    2 cups fresh berries
¼ cup chopped walnuts

1. Preheat oven to 350°F. Spray 9×5-inch loaf pan with nonstick cooking spray.

2. Combine ¼ cup all-purpose flour, oats, brown sugar and butter in small bowl; mix with fork until crumbly.

3. Beat remaining 1 cup all-purpose flour, whole wheat flour, milk, granulated sugar, oil, egg, baking powder, cinnamon and salt in large bowl with electric mixer or whisk 1 to 2 minutes until well blended. Gently fold in berries. Spread batter in prepared pan; sprinkle evenly with oat mixture and walnuts.

4. Bake 38 to 40 minutes or until toothpick inserted into center comes out clean. Serve warm. *Makes 12 servings*

Nutrients per Serving (1 (¾-inch) slice)

Calories: 272, **Total Fat:** 10g, **Saturated Fat:** 3g, **Cholesterol:** 26mg, **Sodium:** 256mg, **Carbohydrate:** 42g, **Fiber:** 3g, **Protein:** 5g

Mixed Berry Whole Grain Coffee Cake

french toast muffins with bananas & peanut butter syrup

½ cup low-fat (1%) milk

2 large egg whites

1 teaspoon vanilla

¼ teaspoon ground nutmeg

4 multigrain or whole wheat English muffins, split

1 teaspoon unsalted butter

1 large banana, peeled and thinly sliced

¼ cup chunky or creamy peanut butter

¼ cup sugar-free maple syrup

1. Preheat oven to 200°F. Whisk milk, egg whites, vanilla and nutmeg in shallow dish or pie plate until well blended. Place 2 split muffins in dish; turn to coat. Let stand 2 minutes.

2. Melt butter in large nonstick skillet over medium heat. Remove muffins from egg mixture, allowing excess to drip off; add to skillet. Place remaining 2 split muffins in egg mixture; turn to coat. Let stand while cooking first batch 2 minutes per side or until golden brown. Transfer to two serving plates; place in oven to keep warm. Repeat with remaining muffins.

3. Sprinkle banana slices over French toast. Place peanut butter in small microwavable bowl; microwave on HIGH 15 to 20 seconds until warm. Gradually stir in syrup until smooth. Drizzle over bananas and French toast. *Makes 4 servings*

Nutrients per Serving (2 pieces French toast and 2 tablespoons syrup)

Calories: 316, **Total Fat:** 10g, **Saturated Fat:** 2g, **Cholesterol:** 4mg, **Sodium:** 422mg, **Carbohydrate:** 45g, **Fiber:** 4g, **Protein:** 13g

fruited granola

3 cups quick oats
1 cup sliced almonds
1 cup honey
½ cup wheat germ or honey wheat germ
3 tablespoons butter or margarine, melted
1 teaspoon ground cinnamon
3 cups whole grain cereal flakes
½ cup dried blueberries or golden raisins
½ cup dried cranberries or cherries
½ cup dried banana chips or chopped pitted dates

1. Preheat oven to 325°F.

2. Spread oats and almonds in single layer in 13×9-inch baking pan. Bake 15 minutes or until lightly toasted, stirring frequently.

3. Combine honey, wheat germ, butter and cinnamon in large bowl until well blended. Add oats and almonds; toss to coat completely. Spread mixture in single layer in baking pan. Bake 20 minutes or until golden brown. Cool completely in pan on wire rack. Break mixture into chunks.

4. Combine oat chunks, cereal, blueberries, cranberries and banana chips in large bowl. Store in airtight container at room temperature up to 2 weeks.

Makes about 20 servings

Tip: Prepare this granola on the weekend and you'll have a scrumptious snack or breakfast treat on hand for the rest of the week!

Nutrients per Serving (½ cup)

Calories: 210, **Total Fat:** 7g, **Saturated Fat:** 2g, **Cholesterol:** 5mg, **Sodium:** 58mg, **Carbohydrate:** 36g, **Fiber:** 4g, **Protein:** 5g

sunny seed bran waffles

2 egg whites

1 tablespoon dark brown sugar

1 tablespoon canola or vegetable oil

1 cup fat-free (skim) milk

⅔ cup unprocessed wheat bran

⅔ cup quick oats

1½ teaspoons baking powder

¼ teaspoon salt

3 tablespoons toasted sunflower seeds*

1 cup apple butter

To toast sunflower seeds, cook and stir in small nonstick skillet over medium heat about 5 minutes or until golden brown, stirring occasionally. Remove from skillet; let cool.

1. Beat egg whites in medium bowl with electric mixer until soft peaks form. Blend brown sugar and oil in small bowl. Stir in milk; mix well.

2. Combine bran, oats, baking powder and salt in large bowl; mix well. Stir sugar mixture into bran mixture. Add sunflower seeds; stir just until moistened. *Do not overmix.* Gently fold in beaten egg whites.

3. Spray nonstick waffle iron lightly with nonstick cooking spray; heat according to manufacturer's directions. Stir batter; spoon ½ cup batter into waffle iron for each waffle. Cook until steam stops escaping from around edges and waffle is golden brown. Serve each waffle with ¼ cup apple butter.   *Makes 4 waffles*

Note: It is essential to use a nonstick waffle iron because of the low fat content of these waffles.

Nutrients per Serving (1 waffle with ¼ cup apple butter)

Calories: 384, **Total Fat:** 10g, **Saturated Fat:** 1g, **Cholesterol:** 1mg, **Sodium:** 318mg, **Carbohydrate:** 68g, **Fiber:** 6g, **Protein:** 12g

Sunny Seed Bran Waffle

morning sandwiches

1 tablespoon butter or vegetable oil
¾ cup quick oats
¼ cup sliced almonds
1 cup whole wheat flour
1 cup peeled and grated apple
1 cup shredded carrots
⅓ cup cholesterol-free egg substitute
¼ cup pitted and chopped prunes
¼ cup fat-free (skim) milk
2 tablespoons sugar substitute or granulated sugar
½ teaspoon baking powder
½ teaspoon ground cinnamon
¼ teaspoon baking soda
¼ teaspoon ground nutmeg
6 teaspoons reduced-fat peanut butter
6 teaspoons sugar-free raspberry preserves

1. Preheat oven to 425°F. Spray 13×9-inch baking pan with nonstick cooking spray.

2. Melt butter in small nonstick saucepan over medium heat. Add oats and almonds; cook and stir 3 minutes. Remove from heat and let cool.

3. Place oat mixture, flour, apple, carrots, egg substitute, prunes, milk, sugar substitute, baking powder, cinnamon, baking soda and nutmeg in food processor; pulse until combined. Press dough evenly into prepared pan.

4. Bake 20 minutes. Cool in pan on wire rack 15 minutes.

5. Cut into 12 pieces. Spread 6 pieces with peanut butter; spread remaining 6 pieces with raspberry preserves. Press pieces together to form sandwiches.

Makes 6 servings

Nutrients per Serving (1 sandwich)

Calories: 272, **Total Fat:** 11g, **Saturated Fat:** 2g, **Cholesterol:** 6mg, **Sodium:** 215mg, **Carbohydrate:** 36g, **Fiber:** 7g, **Protein:** 10g

carb lovers' lunches

chicken, hummus & vegetable wraps

¾ cup hummus (regular, roasted red pepper or roasted garlic)

4 (8- to 10-inch) whole wheat tortillas, sun-dried tomato wraps or spinach wraps

2 cups chopped cooked chicken breast

Chipotle hot pepper sauce or Louisiana-style hot pepper sauce (optional)

½ cup shredded carrots

½ cup chopped unpeeled cucumber

½ cup thinly sliced radishes

2 tablespoons chopped fresh mint or basil

1. Spread hummus evenly over wraps all the way to edges.

2. Place chicken over hummus; sprinkle with hot sauce, if desired. Top with carrots, cucumber, radishes and mint. Roll up tightly. Cut in half diagonally.

Makes 4 servings

Nutrients per Serving (1 wrap)

Calories: 308, **Total Fat:** 10g, **Saturated Fat:** 1g, **Cholesterol:** 60mg, **Sodium:** 540mg, **Carbohydrate:** 32g, **Fiber:** 15g, **Protein:** 32g

one-for-all veggie sub

½ (15-ounce) can navy beans, rinsed and drained
⅓ cup chipotle salsa
1 to 2 tablespoons red wine vinegar
½ to 1 tablespoon dried oregano
1 clove garlic
1 round loaf (16 ounces) multigrain Italian bread
1 medium tomato, thinly sliced
1 cup packed spring greens
½ small red onion, thinly sliced
1 Anaheim chile pepper,* halved and thinly sliced
¾ cup (3 ounces) crumbled reduced-fat feta cheese

*Or substitute 3 ounces thinly sliced green bell pepper for the Anaheim chile pepper.

1. Combine beans, salsa, vinegar, oregano and garlic in food processor; process until smooth.

2. Cut bread in half horizontally, making two rounds. Hollow out top and bottom halves of bread, leaving ½-inch-thick shell; reserve torn bread for another use.

3. Spread bean mixture evenly on cut sides of bread. Arrange tomato slices over bottom half of bread. Top with greens, onion, pepper, cheese and top half of bread. Cut filled loaf into 6 wedges.   *Makes 6 servings*

Nutrients per Serving (1 sandwich wedge)

Calories: 257, **Total Fat:** 3g, **Saturated Fat:** 2g, **Cholesterol:** 4mg, **Sodium:** 614mg, **Carbohydrate:** 45g, **Fiber:** 6g, **Protein:** 13g

couscous primavera

1 shallot, minced *or* ¼ cup minced red onion
8 medium spears fresh asparagus, cooked and cut into 1-inch pieces
1 cup frozen peas
1 cup halved grape tomatoes
½ cup water
⅛ teaspoon salt
⅛ teaspoon black pepper
6 tablespoons uncooked whole wheat couscous
¼ cup grated Parmesan cheese

1. Spray large skillet with nonstick cooking spray. Add shallot; cook over medium-high heat 3 minutes or until tender. Add asparagus and peas; cook 2 minutes or until peas are heated through. Add tomatoes; cook 2 minutes or until softened. Add water, salt and pepper; bring to a boil.

2. Stir in couscous. Reduce heat to low; cover and simmer 2 minutes or until water is absorbed. Fluff with fork and stir in cheese. Serve immediately.   *Makes 2 servings*

Nutrients per Serving (1½ cups)

Calories: 223, **Total Fat:** 4g, **Saturated Fat:** 2g, **Cholesterol:** 9mg, **Sodium:** 363mg, **Carbohydrate:** 38g, **Fiber:** 8g, **Protein:** 14g

instant individual pizza

1 (6-inch) whole wheat tortilla
1 tablespoon no-salt-added tomato sauce *or* 2 teaspoons prepared pesto
¼ teaspoon dried oregano
2 tablespoons shredded reduced-fat Swiss or part-skim mozzarella cheese

1. Preheat oven to 500°F. Place tortilla on baking sheet. Spread tortilla to edges with tomato sauce. Sprinkle with oregano; top with cheese.

2. Bake 5 minutes or until tortilla is crisp and cheese is bubbly.   *Makes 1 serving*

Nutrients per Serving (1 pizza)

Calories: 106, **Total Fat:** 2g, **Saturated Fat:** 1g, **Cholesterol:** 8mg, **Sodium:** 208mg, **Carbohydrate:** 13g, **Fiber:** 9g, **Protein:** 7g

heavenly cranberry turkey sandwiches

¼ cup reduced-fat cream cheese

¼ cup cranberry sauce or chutney

2 tablespoons chopped toasted* walnuts

8 slices multigrain or whole wheat bread, lightly toasted

½ pound sliced deli smoked turkey breast

1 cup packed mesclun or mixed salad greens

To toast walnuts, spread in single layer on baking sheet. Bake in preheated 350°F oven 5 to 7 minutes or until fragrant, stirring occasionally.

1. Combine cream cheese and cranberry sauce in small bowl; mix well. Stir in walnuts.

2. Spread mixture on toast slices. Layer turkey and greens on 4 slices; top with remaining 4 slices. Cut diagonally in half. *Makes 4 servings*

Nutrients per Serving (1 sandwich)

Calories: 291, **Total Fat:** 8g, **Saturated Fat:** 2g, **Cholesterol:** 28mg, **Sodium:** 698mg, **Carbohydrate:** 39g, **Fiber:** 9g, **Protein:** 20g

mediterranean pitas

2 whole wheat pita bread rounds

½ cup roasted red pepper hummus spread

4 slices thinly sliced turkey

¼ medium cucumber, thinly sliced

1 medium red bell pepper, cut into 2-inch-long strips

¼ cup (1 ounce) crumbled reduced-fat feta cheese

½ cup alfalfa sprouts

1. Cut pitas in half and wrap in paper towel; microwave on HIGH 10 seconds.

2. Spread inside of each pita half with 2 tablespoons hummus. Fill each half with turkey, cucumber, bell pepper, cheese and sprouts. *Makes 4 servings*

Nutrients per Serving (½ pita)

Calories: 160, **Total Fat:** 5g, **Saturated Fat:** 1g, **Cholesterol:** 9mg, **Sodium:** 536mg, **Carbohydrate:** 22g, **Fiber:** 4g, **Protein:** 9g

Heavenly Cranberry Turkey Sandwich

greek chickpea salad

4 cups packed baby spinach leaves
1 cup canned chickpeas, rinsed and drained
1 large shallot, thinly sliced
4 pitted kalamata olives, sliced
2 tablespoons crumbled reduced-fat feta cheese
¼ cup plain fat-free Greek yogurt
2 teaspoons white wine vinegar
1 small clove garlic, minced
1 teaspoon olive oil
¼ teaspoon pepper
⅛ teaspoon salt

1. Combine spinach, chickpeas, shallot, olives and cheese in large bowl; toss gently.

2. Whisk yogurt, vinegar, garlic, oil, pepper and salt in small bowl until well blended. Spoon dressing over salad just before serving. Toss gently to coat.

Makes 4 to 5 servings

Nutrients per Serving (1 cup)

Calories: 115, **Total Fat:** 3g, **Saturated Fat:** 1g, **Cholesterol:** 2mg, **Sodium:** 409mg, **Carbohydrate:** 17g, **Fiber:** 4g, **Protein:** 6g

Greek Chickpea Salad

niçoise salad wraps

½ cup bite-size green bean pieces

2 new red potatoes, each cut into 8 wedges

2 tablespoons reduced-fat vinaigrette, divided

1 egg

2 cups watercress leaves

4 ounces water-packed albacore tuna, drained and flaked (about ½ cup)

8 niçoise olives, pitted and halved

3 cherry tomatoes, quartered

2 (10-inch) whole wheat tortillas

1. Bring 8 cups water to a boil in large saucepan. Add green beans and potatoes. Reduce heat to low; simmer 6 minutes or until tender. Remove vegetables with slotted spoon; plunge into ice water to stop cooking. Drain well on paper towels. Transfer to medium bowl; toss with 1 tablespoon vinaigrette.

2. Bring water back to a boil. Add egg; reduce heat and simmer 12 minutes. Cool in ice water. Peel and cut into 8 wedges.

3. Add watercress, tuna, olives, tomatoes and remaining 1 tablespoon vinaigrette to vegetables; toss gently.

4. Heat tortillas in dry nonstick skillet over medium-high heat, turning when softened. Place on plates.

5. Divide salad between tortillas; top with egg wedges. Roll up tortillas to enclose filling. Cut each roll in half before serving.   *Makes 2 servings*

Nutrients per Serving (1 wrap)

Calories: 306, **Total Fat:** 11g, **Saturated Fat:** 1g, **Cholesterol:** 120mg, **Sodium:** 833mg, **Carbohydrate:** 43g, **Fiber:** 18g, **Protein:** 24g

Niçoise Salad Wrap

wilted spinach salad with white beans & olives

  2 thick slices bacon, diced
½ cup chopped onion
  1 can (about 15 ounces) navy beans, rinsed and drained
½ cup halved pitted kalamata or black olives
  1 package (9 ounces) baby spinach
  1 cup cherry tomatoes (cut in half if large)
1½ tablespoons balsamic vinegar
     Black pepper (optional)

1. Cook bacon in large saucepan over medium heat 2 minutes. Add onion; cook 5 to 6 minutes or until bacon is crisp and onion is tender, stirring occasionally. Stir in beans and olives; heat through.

2. Add spinach, tomatoes and vinegar; cover and cook 1 minute or until spinach is slightly wilted. Turn off heat; toss lightly. Transfer to serving plates. Season with pepper, if desired. *Makes 4 servings*

Nutrients per Serving (1¾ cups)

Calories: 230, **Total Fat:** 5g, **Saturated Fat:** 1g, **Cholesterol:** 5mg, **Sodium:** 324mg, **Carbohydrate:** 35g, **Fiber:** 14g, **Protein:** 13g

Beans are a dieter's best friend, providing 12 to 19 grams of fiber per cup. They are a source of both soluble and insoluble fiber, helping to absorb water, fill you up and keep your blood sugar levels stable.

cucumber cheese melts

1 ounce fat-free cream cheese, softened
1 tablespoon crumbled blue cheese
4 slices multigrain bread
2 tablespoons sugar-free apricot fruit spread
8 cucumber slices
1 ounce shaved reduced-sodium ham
2 slices (1½ ounces) fat-free Swiss cheese
   Butter-flavored cooking spray

1. Mix cream cheese and blue cheese in small bowl until well blended. Spread on 2 bread slices. Spread 1 tablespoon apricot fruit spread over cheese mixture on each slice. Top each with cucumber slices, ham, Swiss cheese and remaining bread slices.

2. Lightly spray medium skillet with cooking spray; heat over medium heat. Cook sandwiches over medium heat 4 minutes or until bottoms are browned. Spray tops of sandwiches with cooking spray. Turn and cook 4 minutes or until browned.

3. Cut sandwiches into 4 slices before serving, if desired.   *Makes 2 servings*

Nutrients per Serving (1 sandwich)

Calories: 246, **Total Fat:** 5g, **Saturated Fat:** 1g, **Cholesterol:** 12mg, **Sodium:** 743mg, **Carbohydrate:** 40g, **Fiber:** 8g, **Protein:** 17g

Cucumber Cheese Melt

mediterranean barley salad

1⅓ cups water

⅔ cup quick-cooking barley

½ cup diced roasted red peppers

12 pitted kalamata olives, coarsely chopped

12 turkey pepperoni slices, halved

¼ cup chopped red onion

2 ounces crumbled low-fat feta cheese

1 teaspoon dried basil

¼ teaspoon dried red pepper flakes

1 can (16 ounces) low-sodium navy beans

1 can (14 ounces) sliced hearts of palm, drained

1 tablespoon extra virgin olive oil

1 tablespoon cider vinegar

Salt and black pepper (optional)

1. Bring water to a boil in medium saucepan over high heat. Add barley; return to a boil. Reduce heat to low; cover and simmer 15 minutes or until barley is tender.

2. Meanwhile, combine roasted peppers, olives, pepperoni, onion, cheese, basil and red pepper flakes in medium bowl.

3. Place barley and beans in colander; run under cold water until barley is cool and beans are rinsed. Add barley, beans, hearts of palm, oil and vinegar to roasted pepper mixture; toss gently to blend.

4. Season with salt and pepper, if desired. Refrigerate until ready to serve.

Makes 4 servings

Nutrients per Serving (1½ cups)

Calories: 370, **Total Fat:** 9g, **Saturated Fat:** 2g, **Cholesterol:** 12mg, **Sodium:** 1,013mg, **Carbohydrate:** 57g, **Fiber:** 12g, **Protein:** 20g

Mediterranean Barley Salad

fresh spinach & couscous salad with feta

1 cup water
¾ cup uncooked whole wheat couscous
½ (15-ounce) can white beans, rinsed and drained
1 cup coarsely chopped spinach leaves, packed
1 can (2¼ ounces) sliced black olives, drained
3 slices (1 ounce) hard salami, cut into thin strips
3 tablespoons fat-free vinaigrette
3 tablespoons cider vinegar
1 tablespoon dried oregano
1½ teaspoons dried basil
⅛ teaspoon red pepper flakes
3 ounces feta cheese with sun-dried tomatoes and basil

Microwave Directions

1. Microwave water in medium microwavable bowl on HIGH 2 to 3 minutes or until boiling. Stir in couscous. Cover with plastic wrap; let stand 5 minutes or until water is absorbed.

2. Place couscous in fine mesh strainer. Rinse under cold water until cool; drain.

3. Combine beans, spinach, olives, salami, vinaigrette, vinegar, oregano, basil and red pepper flakes in large bowl.

4. Add couscous to spinach mixture; stir until blended. Add cheese; toss gently.

Makes 4 servings

Tip: To cool couscous quickly, fluff with a fork, spread in a thin layer on a baking sheet and let stand 5 minutes.

Nutrients per Serving (1½ cups)

Calories: 335, **Total Fat:** 10g, **Saturated Fat:** 4g, **Cholesterol:** 21mg, **Sodium:** 622mg, **Carbohydrate:** 50g, **Fiber:** 9g, **Protein:** 16g

shrimp, chickpea & tabouleh pockets

1 package (7 ounces) prepared tabouleh*
¼ pound cooked small shrimp, tails removed, chopped
1 cup diced tomatoes
1 cup canned chickpeas, rinsed and drained
2 whole wheat pita bread rounds

Prepared tabouleh can be found in most grocery stores. It is usually located near the refrigerated hummus and salsa. If you can't find prepared tabouleh, you may use a 5- or 6-ounce package tabouleh mix prepared according to package directions, omitting any extra salt or fat.

1. Combine tabouleh, shrimp, tomatoes and chickpeas in medium bowl; mix well.

2. Cut pitas in half and wrap in paper towel; microwave on HIGH 10 seconds. Fill pita halves evenly with tabouleh mixture.   *Makes 4 servings*

Nutrients per Serving (1 pita half with about 1 cup filling)

Calories: 234, **Total Fat:** 6g, **Saturated Fat:** 1g, **Cholesterol:** 55mg, **Sodium:** 527mg, **Carbohydrate:** 34g, **Fiber:** 7g, **Protein:** 14g

5-minute heat 'n' go soup

1 can (about 15 ounces) no-salt-added navy beans, rinsed and drained
1 can (about 14 ounces) diced tomatoes with green peppers and onions
1 cup water
1½ teaspoons dried basil
½ teaspoon sugar
½ teaspoon chicken bouillon granules
2 teaspoons olive oil

Place all ingredients except oil in medium saucepan; bring to a boil over high heat. Reduce heat and simmer 5 minutes. Remove from heat; stir in oil.

Makes 4 servings

Nutrients per Serving (about ¾ cup)

Calories: 148, **Total Fat:** 3g, **Saturated Fat:** <1g, **Cholesterol:** <1mg, **Sodium:** 451mg, **Carbohydrate:** 25g, **Fiber:** 8g, **Protein:** 7g

Shrimp, Chickpea & Tabouleh Pocket

soups & chilis

greens, white bean & barley soup

2 tablespoons olive oil

3 carrots, diced

1½ cups chopped onions

2 cloves garlic, minced

1½ cups sliced mushrooms

6 cups vegetable broth

2 cups cooked barley

1 can (about 15 ounces) Great Northern beans, rinsed and drained

2 bay leaves

1 teaspoon sugar

1 teaspoon dried thyme

7 cups chopped stemmed collard greens (about 24 ounces)

1 tablespoon white wine vinegar

Hot pepper sauce

Red bell pepper strips (optional)

1. Heat oil in Dutch oven or large saucepan over medium heat. Add carrots, onions and garlic; cook and stir 3 minutes. Add mushrooms; cook and stir 5 minutes or until carrots are tender.

2. Stir in broth, barley, beans, bay leaves, sugar and thyme; bring to a boil over high heat. Reduce heat to medium-low; cover and simmer 5 minutes. Add greens; simmer 10 minutes.

3. Remove and discard bay leaves. Stir in vinegar; season with hot pepper sauce. Garnish with red bell peppers. *Makes 8 servings*

Nutrients per Serving (1¼ cups)

Calories: 226, **Total Fat:** 4g, **Saturated Fat:** .6g, **Cholesterol:** 0mg, **Sodium:** 510mg, **Carbohydrate:** 36g, **Fiber:** 8g, **Protein:** 9g

fresh tomato chili

1 tablespoon olive oil

1 small onion, chopped (about 1 cup)

1 clove garlic, minced

1 medium tomato, diced (about 1½ cups)

1 cup frozen corn

1 can (8 ounces) tomato sauce

1 cup canned kidney beans, rinsed and drained

½ to ⅔ cup reduced-sodium chicken or vegetable broth, divided

1 teaspoon chili powder

½ teaspoon ground cumin

¼ teaspoon dried oregano

⅛ teaspoon salt

⅛ teaspoon black pepper

⅛ teaspoon red pepper flakes

1 cup water

1 cup uncooked instant brown rice

1. Heat oil in large nonstick skillet or saucepan over medium-high heat. Add onion and garlic; cook and stir 5 minutes. Add tomato and corn; cook and stir 3 minutes.

2. Add tomato sauce, beans, ½ cup broth, chili powder, cumin, oregano, salt, black pepper and red pepper flakes; simmer 6 to 8 minutes. Add remaining broth if chili is too thick.

3. Meanwhile, bring water to a boil in small saucepan over high heat. Add rice. Reduce heat to low; cover and simmer 5 minutes. Remove from heat; let stand 5 minutes. Fluff with fork. Serve chili over rice.   *Makes 4 servings*

Nutrients per Serving (¾ cup chili with ⅓ cup rice)

Calories: 293, **Total Fat:** 2g, **Saturated Fat:** <1g, **Cholesterol:** <1mg, **Sodium:** 245mg, **Carbohydrate:** 61g, **Fiber:** 9g, **Protein:** 11g

Fresh Tomato Chili

italian skillet roasted vegetable soup

2 tablespoons olive oil, divided

1 medium yellow, red or orange bell pepper, chopped

1 clove garlic, minced

2 cups water

1 can (about 14 ounces) diced tomatoes

1 medium zucchini, thinly sliced

⅛ teaspoon red pepper flakes

1 can (about 15 ounces) navy beans, rinsed and drained

3 to 4 tablespoons chopped fresh basil

1 tablespoon balsamic vinegar

½ teaspoon liquid smoke (optional)

¾ teaspoon salt

1. Heat 1 tablespoon oil in Dutch oven or large saucepan over medium-high heat. Add bell pepper; cook and stir 4 minutes or until edges are browned. Add garlic; cook and stir 15 seconds.

2. Stir in water, tomatoes, zucchini and red pepper flakes; bring to a boil over high heat. Reduce heat to low; cover and simmer 20 minutes.

3. Add beans, basil, remaining 1 tablespoon oil, vinegar, liquid smoke, if desired, and salt. Remove from heat. Let stand, covered, 10 minutes before serving.

Makes 5 servings

Tip: Serve with croutons, if desired.

Nutrients per Serving (1 cup)

Calories: 157, **Total Fat:** 3g, **Saturated Fat:** <1g, **Cholesterol:** 0mg, **Sodium:** 670mg, **Carbohydrate:** 25g, **Fiber:** 6g, **Protein:** 8g

middle eastern lentil soup

1 cup dried lentils
2 tablespoons olive oil
1 small onion, chopped
1 medium red bell pepper, chopped
1 teaspoon whole fennel seeds
½ teaspoon ground cumin
¼ teaspoon ground red pepper
4 cups water
½ teaspoon salt
1 tablespoon lemon juice
½ cup plain low-fat yogurt
2 tablespoons chopped fresh parsley

1. Rinse and drain lentils, discarding any debris or blemished lentils.

2. Heat oil in large saucepan over medium-high heat. Add onion and bell pepper; cook and stir 5 minutes or until tender. Add fennel seeds, cumin and ground red pepper; cook and stir 1 minute.

3. Stir in water, lentils and salt; bring to a boil over high heat. Reduce heat to low; cover and simmer 25 to 30 minutes or until lentils are tender. Stir in lemon juice.

4. Ladle soup into individual bowls. Top with yogurt; sprinkle with parsley.

Makes 4 servings

Nutrients per Serving (1 cup)
_____

Calories: 266, **Total Fat:** 8g, **Saturated Fat:** 1g, **Cholesterol:** 2mg, **Sodium:** 320mg, **Carbohydrate:** 35g, **Fiber:** 16g, **Protein:** 16g

vegetable & barley chili

⅔ cup water

⅓ cup quick-cooking barley

1 clove garlic, minced

1 small red onion, finely chopped

2 medium tomatoes, coarsely chopped

2 cups frozen Italian-style mixed vegetables

1 can (8 ounces) no-salt-added tomato sauce

1 can (5½ ounces) low-sodium vegetable juice

1½ teaspoons chili powder

½ teaspoon dried oregano

¼ teaspoon ground cumin

¼ plus ⅛ teaspoon salt

⅛ teaspoon black pepper

⅛ teaspoon red pepper flakes

1. Bring water to a boil in small saucepan over high heat; stir in barley. Reduce heat to low; cover and simmer 10 minutes or until barley is tender. Remove from heat; let stand, covered, 5 minutes. Drain any remaining liquid.

2. Meanwhile, spray large nonstick skillet with nonstick cooking spray. Add garlic and onion; cook and stir over medium-high heat 5 minutes or until tender. Add tomatoes; cook over medium heat 3 minutes. Stir in frozen vegetables; cook 2 to 3 minutes or until heated through, stirring occasionally.

3. Stir in drained barley, tomato sauce, vegetable juice, chili powder, oregano, cumin, salt, black pepper and red pepper flakes; cover and simmer 10 minutes.

Makes 3 servings

Note: Italian-style mixed vegetables include zucchini, yellow squash, green beans and carrots.

Nutrients per Serving (1 cup)

Calories: 194, **Total Fat:** 1g, **Saturated Fat:** <1g, **Cholesterol:** 0mg, **Sodium:** 397mg, **Carbohydrate:** 40g, **Fiber:** 9g, **Protein:** 8g

ravioli minestrone

1 package (7 ounces) refrigerated 3-cheese ravioli *or* 1 package (9 ounces) reduced-fat 4-cheese ravioli

2 teaspoons olive oil

2 carrots, chopped

1 medium onion, chopped

1 stalk celery, chopped

2 cloves garlic, minced

6 cups water

1 can (about 15 ounces) chickpeas, rinsed and drained

1 can (about 14 ounces) diced tomatoes

3 tablespoons tomato paste

1 teaspoon dried basil

1 teaspoon dried oregano

¾ teaspoon salt

¾ teaspoon black pepper

1 medium zucchini, cut in half lengthwise and sliced (about 2 cups)

1 package (10 ounces) baby spinach

1. Cook ravioli according to package directions. Drain and keep warm.

2. Meanwhile, heat oil in Dutch oven or large saucepan over medium-high heat. Add carrots, onion, celery and garlic; cook about 5 minutes or until vegetables are softened, stirring occasionally.

3. Stir in water, chickpeas, tomatoes, tomato paste, basil, oregano, salt and pepper; bring to a boil over high heat. Reduce heat to low; simmer 15 minutes or until vegetables are tender. Add zucchini; cook 5 minutes. Stir in spinach; cook 2 minutes or just until wilted. Stir in ravioli. *Makes 8 servings*

Nutrients per Serving (1½ cups)

Calories: 213, **Total Fat:** 6g, **Saturated Fat:** 3g, **Cholesterol:** 19mg, **Sodium:** 516mg, **Carbohydrate:** 33g, **Fiber:** 6g, **Protein:** 8g

zesty vegetarian chili

1 tablespoon canola or vegetable oil

1 large red bell pepper, coarsely chopped

2 medium zucchini or yellow squash (or 1 of each), cut into ½-inch chunks

4 cloves garlic, minced

1 can (about 14 ounces) fire-roasted diced tomatoes

¾ cup chunky salsa

2 teaspoons chili powder

1 teaspoon dried oregano

1 can (about 15 ounces) no-salt-added red kidney beans, rinsed and drained

10 ounces extra-firm tofu, well drained and cut into ½-inch cubes

Chopped cilantro (optional)

1. Heat oil in large saucepan over medium heat. Add bell pepper; cook and stir 4 minutes. Add zucchini and garlic; cook and stir 3 minutes.

2. Stir in tomatoes, salsa, chili powder and oregano; bring to a boil over high heat. Reduce heat to low; simmer 15 minutes or until vegetables are tender.

3. Stir beans into chili. Simmer 2 minutes or until heated through. Stir in tofu; remove from heat. Ladle into shallow bowls; sprinkle with chopped cilantro, if desired.
Makes 4 servings

Note: Tofu has a bland, slightly nutty taste, but it readily takes on the flavor of foods it's cooked with. It's available in three forms: soft, firm, and extra-firm. Cover leftover tofu with water and refrigerate.

Nutrients per Serving (1½ cups)

Calories: 231, **Total Fat:** 8g, **Saturated Fat:** 1g, **Cholesterol:** 0mg, **Sodium:** 432mg, **Carbohydrate:** 28g, **Fiber:** 8g, **Protein:** 15g

smoky navy bean soup

2½ tablespoons olive oil, divided

4 ounces Canadian bacon or extra-lean ham, diced

1 cup diced onion

1 carrot, thinly sliced

1 stalk celery, thinly sliced

3 cups water

6 ounces red potatoes, diced

2 bay leaves

¼ teaspoon dried tarragon

1 can (about 15 ounces) navy beans, rinsed and drained

1½ teaspoons liquid smoke

½ teaspoon salt (optional)

½ teaspoon black pepper

1. Heat 1 tablespoon oil in large saucepan over medium-high heat. Add Canadian bacon; cook and stir 2 minutes or until browned. Remove to paper towel-lined plate.

2. Add onion, carrot and celery to saucepan; spray with nonstick cooking spray. Cook and stir 4 minutes or until onion is translucent. Add water; bring to a boil. Stir in potatoes, bay leaves and tarragon. Reduce heat to medium-low; cover and simmer 20 minutes or until potatoes are tender. Remove from heat.

3. Stir in beans, bacon, remaining 1½ tablespoons oil, liquid smoke, salt, if desired, and pepper; heat through. Remove and discard bay leaves before serving.

Makes 6 servings

Nutrients per Serving (1 cup)

Calories: 177, **Total Fat:** 5g, **Saturated Fat:** <1g, **Cholesterol:** 9mg, **Sodium:** 599mg, **Carbohydrate:** 23g, **Fiber:** 5g, **Protein:** 10g

Smoky Navy Bean Soup

ground beef, spinach & barley soup

¾ pound 95% lean ground beef

4 cups water

1 can (about 14 ounces) stewed tomatoes

1½ cups thinly sliced carrots

1 cup chopped onion

½ cup quick-cooking barley

1½ teaspoons beef bouillon granules

1½ teaspoons dried thyme

1 teaspoon dried oregano

½ teaspoon garlic powder

¼ teaspoon black pepper

⅛ teaspoon salt

3 cups torn stemmed spinach leaves

1. Brown beef in large saucepan over medium-high heat 6 to 8 minutes, stirring to break up meat. Rinse beef under warm water; drain.

2. Return beef to saucepan. Stir in water, tomatoes, carrots, onion, barley, bouillon granules, thyme, oregano, garlic powder, pepper and salt; bring to a boil over high heat. Reduce heat to medium-low; cover and simmer 12 to 15 minutes or until barley and vegetables are tender, stirring occasionally.

3. Stir in spinach; cook just until spinach begins to wilt.   *Makes 4 servings*

Nutrients per Serving

Calories: 265, **Total Fat:** 6g, **Saturated Fat:** 2g, **Cholesterol:** 22mg, **Sodium:** 512mg, **Carbohydrate:** 33g, **Fiber:** 8g, **Protein:** 22g

southwest corn & turkey soup

2 dried ancho chiles (each about 4 inches long) *or* 6 dried New Mexico chiles (each about 6 inches long)*

1 medium onion, thinly sliced

3 cloves garlic, minced

1 teaspoon ground cumin

3 cans (about 14 ounces each) fat-free reduced-sodium chicken broth

2 small zucchini, cut in half lengthwise, then crosswise into ½-inch slices

1½ to 2 cups shredded cooked turkey

1 can (about 15 ounces) black beans or chickpeas, rinsed and drained

1 package (10 ounces) frozen corn

¼ cup cornmeal

1 teaspoon dried oregano

⅓ cup chopped fresh cilantro

Chile peppers can sting and irritate the skin, so wear rubber gloves when handling peppers and do not touch your eyes.

1. Cut stems from chiles; shake out seeds. Place chiles in medium bowl; cover with boiling water. Let stand 20 to 40 minutes or until chiles are soft; drain. Cut open lengthwise and lay flat on work surface. Scrape chile pulp from skin with edge of small knife. Finely mince pulp; set aside.

2. Spray large saucepan with nonstick cooking spray; heat over medium heat. Add onion; cover and cook 4 minutes or until light golden brown, stirring occasionally. Add garlic and cumin; cook and stir about 30 seconds or until fragrant.

3. Stir in broth, reserved chile pulp, zucchini, turkey, beans, corn, cornmeal and oregano; bring to a boil over high heat. Reduce heat to low; simmer, uncovered, 15 minutes or until zucchini is tender. Stir in cilantro.   *Makes 6 servings*

Nutrients per Serving (about 1½ cups)

Calories: 243, **Total Fat:** 5g, **Saturated Fat:** 1g, **Cholesterol:** 32mg, **Sodium:** 408mg, **Carbohydrate:** 32g, **Fiber:** 7g, **Protein:** 19g

Southwest Corn & Turkey Soup

lentil chili

1 tablespoon canola oil

4 cloves garlic, minced

1 tablespoon chili powder

1 package (32 ounces) reduced-sodium vegetable broth

¾ cup dried brown or green lentils, rinsed and drained

2 teaspoons smoked chipotle hot pepper sauce

2 cups peeled and diced butternut squash

1 can (about 14 ounces) no-salt-added diced tomatoes

½ cup chopped fresh cilantro

¼ cup pepitas* (optional)

Pepitas are roasted pumpkin seeds often used in Mexican cooking. You can find them in the ethnic section of many supermarkets or in Mexican or specialty food stores.

1. Heat oil in large saucepan over medium heat. Add garlic; cook and stir 1 minute. Stir in chili powder; cook and stir 30 seconds.

2. Stir in broth, lentils and hot pepper sauce; bring to a boil over high heat. Reduce heat to low; simmer 15 minutes. Stir in squash and tomatoes; simmer 18 to 20 minutes or until lentils and squash are tender.

3. Ladle into bowls; top with cilantro and pepitas, if desired.   *Makes 5 servings*

Note: Lentils are not only a good source of iron and protein, but are packed with dietary fiber. The soluble fiber in lentils helps to stabilize blood sugar levels while the insoluble fiber is known to lower high cholesterol levels and promote digestive health.

Nutrients per Serving (1 cup)

Calories: 184, **Total Fat:** 3g, **Saturated Fat:** <1g, **Cholesterol:** 0mg, **Sodium:** 322mg, **Carbohydrate:** 32g, **Fiber:** 12g, **Protein:** 10g

no-guilt pasta

mediterranean veggies with beans & penne

4 ounces uncooked multigrain penne pasta
1 can (about 15 ounces) no-salt-added navy beans, rinsed and drained
1 medium green bell pepper, chopped
1 small zucchini, sliced
2 cloves garlic, minced
1 can (about 14 ounces) stewed tomatoes, undrained
2 teaspoons dried basil
2 teaspoons extra virgin olive oil
½ cup (2 ounces) shredded mozzarella cheese
1 tablespoon plus 1 teaspoon grated Parmesan cheese

1. Cook pasta according to package directions, omitting salt and fat. Add beans during last minute of cooking. Drain and keep warm.

2. Meanwhile, spray large nonstick skillet with nonstick cooking spray; heat over medium-high heat. Add bell peppers and zucchini; cook and stir 5 minutes or until edges of vegetables begin to brown. Add garlic; cook and stir 15 seconds.

3. Stir in tomatoes and basil; bring to a boil over high heat. Reduce heat to low; cover and simmer 10 minutes. Stir in oil.

4. Spoon tomato mixture over pasta and beans; sprinkle with cheeses.

Makes 5 servings

Nutrients per Serving (about 1 cup)

Calories: 296, **Total Fat:** 6g, **Saturated Fat:** 2g, **Cholesterol:** 7mg, **Sodium:** 376mg, **Carbohydrate:** 48g, **Fiber:** 13g, **Protein:** 16g

peanut-sauced pasta

9 ounces uncooked multigrain linguine

1½ pounds fresh asparagus, cut into 1-inch pieces (4 cups)

⅓ cup vegetable broth

3 tablespoons creamy peanut butter

2 tablespoons seasoned rice vinegar

2 tablespoons reduced-sodium soy sauce

½ teaspoon red pepper flakes

⅓ cup unsalted dry-roasted peanuts, chopped

1. Cook pasta according to package directions, omitting salt and fat. Add asparagus during last 5 minutes of cooking.

2. Meanwhile, combine broth, peanut butter, vinegar, soy sauce and red pepper flakes in small saucepan; cook over low heat until heated through, stirring frequently.

3. Drain pasta and asparagus; toss with warm peanut sauce. Sprinkle with peanuts.

Makes 6 servings

Nutrients per Serving (1 cup)

Calories: 300, **Total Fat:** 11g, **Saturated Fat:** 2g, **Cholesterol:** 0mg, **Sodium:** 449mg, **Carbohydrate:** 38g, **Fiber:** 5g, **Protein:** 14g

Multigrain pastas contain dense flours such as quinoa or amaranth, which makes them richer in protein. They contain slightly less fiber per serving than whole grain pastas (4 grams for multigrain versus 7 for whole grain), but they also provide a number of other essential vitamins and nutrients, making them a very healthy option.

rotini with spinach & beans

8 cups fresh spinach, stemmed and leaves torn

4 cups hot cooked multigrain or whole wheat rotini pasta

1 can (about 15 ounces) cannellini beans, rinsed and drained

½ cup grated Romano cheese

2 tablespoons olive oil

2 cloves garlic, minced

¼ teaspoon salt

¼ teaspoon black pepper

Combine all ingredients in large bowl; mix well.   *Makes 8 servings*

Nutrients per Serving (1¼ cups)

Calories: 190, **Total Fat:** 6g, **Saturated Fat:** 2g, **Cholesterol:** 7mg,
Sodium: 313mg, **Carbohydrate:** 28g, **Fiber:** 5g, **Protein:** 10g

greek pasta salad

6 cups cooked multigrain or whole wheat rotini or penne pasta

1½ cups diced cucumber

2 medium tomatoes, diced

1 medium green bell pepper, diced

2 ounces feta cheese, finely crumbled

12 medium pitted black olives, sliced into thirds

¼ cup chopped fresh dill

Juice of ½ lemon

¼ teaspoon salt

⅛ teaspoon black pepper

Combine all ingredients in large bowl; toss to coat. Refrigerate until ready to serve.
Makes 8 servings

Nutrients per Serving (1 cup)

Calories: 202, **Total Fat:** 4g, **Saturated Fat:** 1g, **Cholesterol:** 8mg,
Sodium: 218mg, **Carbohydrate:** 35g, **Fiber:** 5g, **Protein:** 7g

Rotini with Spinach & Beans

pasta putanesca

1 tablespoon olive oil

½ cup chopped onion

2 teaspoons capers, rinsed and drained

1 clove garlic, minced

1 teaspoon Italian seasoning

1 bay leaf

 Pinch red pepper flakes or few drops hot pepper sauce (optional)

1 can (about 14 ounces) diced tomatoes

1 can (6 ounces) water-packed solid white albacore tuna, drained

¼ cup pitted kalamata olives

3 tablespoons chopped fresh Italian flat leaf parsley *or* 1 tablespoon
  dried parsley flakes

 Juice of ½ lemon

2 cups hot cooked multigrain spaghetti

¼ cup grated Parmesan cheese

1. Heat oil in large skillet over medium heat. Add onion; cook and stir about 2 minutes or until translucent. Add capers, garlic, Italian seasoning, bay leaf and red pepper flakes, if desired; cook and stir about 1 minute or until aromatic.

2. Add tomatoes, tuna and olives, stirring to break up tuna into chunks. Cook about 5 minutes or until heated through. Just before serving, stir in parsley and lemon juice.

3. Divide pasta between four serving bowls; top with sauce. Sprinkle each serving with 1 tablespoon cheese. *Makes 4 servings*

Nutrients per Serving (¾ cup sauce and ½ cup pasta with 1 tablespoon cheese)

Calories: 321, **Total Fat:** 8g, **Saturated Fat:** 1g, **Cholesterol:** 15mg, **Sodium:** 787mg, **Carbohydrate:** 44g, **Fiber:** 5g, **Protein:** 20g

curried chicken & vegetable noodle bowl

6 ounces uncooked whole wheat egg noodles

¾ pound boneless skinless chicken breasts or chicken tenders, cut into ¾-inch chunks

2 tablespoons all-purpose flour

2 teaspoons curry powder

½ teaspoon salt

¼ teaspoon red pepper flakes (optional)

1 tablespoon canola oil

1 cup reduced-sodium chicken broth

12 ounces frozen mixed vegetable medley such as broccoli, cauliflower and red bell peppers, thawed and drained

2 tablespoons sliced almonds

1. Cook noodles according to package directions, omitting salt and fat.

2. Meanwhile, combine chicken, flour, curry powder, salt and red pepper flakes, if desired, in medium bowl; toss to coat.

3. Heat oil in large saucepan or large deep skillet over medium heat. Add chicken mixture; cook and stir 3 to 4 minutes or until chicken loses pink color. Stir in broth and vegetables; bring to a boil. Reduce heat to low; simmer, uncovered, about 8 minutes or until chicken is cooked through and sauce is slightly thickened. Serve over hot cooked noodles in shallow bowls. Top with almonds.

Makes 6 servings

Nutrients per Serving (¾ cup noodles with 1 cup chicken mixture)

Calories: 328, **Total Fat:** 8g, **Saturated Fat:** 2g, **Cholesterol:** 73mg, **Sodium:** 409mg, **Carbohydrate:** 33g, **Fiber:** 6g, **Protein:** 31g

mediterranean pasta salad

½ (14½-ounce) package uncooked multigrain or whole wheat rigatoni
   or penne pasta
½ cup balsamic, white balsamic or red wine vinegar
3 tablespoons olive oil
2 cloves garlic, minced
1 can (14 ounces) artichoke hearts in water, drained and cut into quarters
½ cup oil-packed sun-dried tomatoes, drained and chopped
½ cup chopped or sliced black olives
4 ounces feta cheese with sun-dried tomatoes and basil
¼ cup chopped fresh basil
3 cups fresh baby spinach, stems removed and leaves torn
¼ cup toasted pine nuts (optional)

1. Cook pasta according to package directions, omitting salt and fat; drain.

2. Meanwhile, combine vinegar, oil and garlic in small jar; cover and shake well to blend.

3. Combine drained pasta, artichokes, tomatoes, olives, cheese and basil in large bowl.

4. Add spinach and dressing to salad just before serving; toss gently to coat. Sprinkle with pine nuts, if desired.   *Makes 8 servings*

Tip: To toast pine nuts, place them in a small skillet over medium heat; cook and stir 1 to 2 minutes or until lightly browned. Immediately remove from skillet to cool.

Nutrients per Serving (1¼ cups)

Calories: 185, **Total Fat:** 10g, **Saturated Fat:** 3g, **Cholesterol:** 10mg, **Sodium:** 307mg, **Carbohydrate:** 21g, **Fiber:** 5g, **Protein:** 6g

macaroni & cheese with mixed vegetables

1¼ cups fat-free (skim) milk, divided

2 tablespoons all-purpose flour

½ cup (2 ounces) shredded reduced-fat sharp Cheddar cheese

½ cup (2 ounces) grated Parmesan cheese

1½ cups frozen mixed vegetables, cooked according to package directions and drained

1⅓ cups cooked whole wheat elbow macaroni, rotini or penne pasta

¼ teaspoon salt (optional)

⅛ teaspoon black pepper

1. Preheat oven to 325°F. Spray 1½-quart baking dish with nonstick cooking spray.

2. Stir ¼ cup milk and flour in medium saucepan until smooth. Add remaining 1 cup milk; stir until well blended. Cook over medium heat until thickened, stirring constantly.

3. Combine Cheddar and Parmesan cheeses in small bowl. Stir half of cheese into saucepan; mix well. Stir in vegetables, macaroni, salt, if desired, and pepper. Spoon macaroni mixture into prepared baking dish; sprinkle with remaining cheese.

4. Bake 20 minutes or until cheese melts and macaroni is heated through. Let stand 5 minutes before serving.   *Makes 4 servings*

Nutrients per Serving (¾ cup)

Calories: 240, **Total Fat:** 6g, **Saturated Fat:** 4g, **Cholesterol:** 20mg, **Sodium:** 330mg, **Carbohydrate:** 32g, **Fiber:** 5g, **Protein:** 15g

pasta with spring vegetables

¼ cup olive oil

½ cup chopped onion

2 cloves garlic, minced

1 pound asparagus, cut into 1-inch pieces

2½ cups cherry tomatoes (12 ounces), halved

2 cups diced yellow squash

¾ cup fat-free reduced-sodium chicken broth

¼ teaspoon salt

¼ teaspoon black pepper

6 cups hot cooked whole wheat or multigrain penne pasta

1½ cups low-sodium marinara sauce

6 fresh basil leaves, cut into thin strips

¼ cup grated Parmesan cheese (optional)

1. Heat oil in large saucepan over medium heat. Add onion and garlic; cook and stir 3 minutes. Add asparagus; cook and stir 4 minutes. Add tomatoes and squash; cook and stir 3 minutes or until tomatoes are softened.

2. Stir in broth. Reduce heat to low; simmer 6 minutes or until asparagus is tender. Season with salt and pepper.

3. Add pasta, marinara sauce and basil to tomato mixture; stir gently to coat. Top with cheese, if desired. *Makes 8 servings*

Nutrients per Serving (1¼ cups)

Calories: 253, **Total Fat:** 9g, **Saturated Fat:** 1g, **Cholesterol:** 0mg, **Sodium:** 285mg, **Carbohydrate:** 37g, **Fiber:** 6g, **Protein:** 8g

white bean & orzo salad

¾ cup uncooked orzo pasta (6 ounces)

1 can (about 15 ounces) reduced-sodium navy beans, rinsed and drained

1 cup packed spinach leaves, coarsely chopped

½ cup chopped roasted bell peppers

3 tablespoons capers, drained and rinsed

3 tablespoons chopped fresh basil

3 tablespoons reduced-fat Italian dressing

¼ cup crumbled feta cheese

Cook pasta according to package directions, omitting salt and fat. Combine beans, spinach, roasted peppers, capers, basil and dressing in large bowl. Drain pasta; add to bean mixture. Add cheese; toss gently to blend.   *Makes 6 servings*

Nutrients per Serving (1 cup)

Calories: 234, **Total Fat:** 2g, **Saturated Fat:** <1g, **Cholesterol:** 4mg, **Sodium:** 336mg, **Carbohydrate:** 43g, **Fiber:** 9g, **Protein:** 11g

pasta with avocado & bell pepper

1 ripe avocado, diced

1 medium red or green bell pepper, diced

½ cup oil-packed sun-dried tomatoes, drained and chopped

½ cup chopped fresh basil

2 green onions, chopped

2 tablespoons olive oil

6 cups hot cooked multigrain or whole wheat penne or rotini pasta

¼ teaspoon salt

¼ teaspoon black pepper

Combine avocado, bell pepper, tomatoes, basil, green onions and oil in large bowl. Add pasta, salt and pepper; toss gently to blend.   *Makes 6 servings*

Nutrients per Serving (1¼ cups)

Calories: 300, **Total Fat:** 12g, **Saturated Fat:** 2g, **Cholesterol:** 0mg, **Sodium:** 128mg, **Carbohydrate:** 45g, **Fiber:** 8g, **Protein:** 9g

White Bean & Orzo Salad

santa fe rotini

3 ounces uncooked whole grain rotini pasta

½ (15-ounce) can black beans, rinsed and drained

⅓ cup finely chopped red onion

1 medium jalapeño pepper,* seeded and chopped

¾ cup quartered grape tomatoes

1 tablespoon extra virgin olive oil

½ medium lime, cut into 4 wedges

1 clove garlic, minced

⅛ teaspoon salt

1 to 2 tablespoons chopped fresh cilantro

Jalapeño peppers can sting and irritate the skin, so wear rubber gloves when handling peppers and do not touch your eyes.

1. Cook pasta according to package directions, omitting salt and fat. Add beans during last minute of cooking.

2. Meanwhile, spray small nonstick skillet with nonstick cooking spray; heat over medium-high heat. Add onion and jalapeño; cook and stir 2 minutes. Add tomatoes; cook and stir 2 minutes or just until tender. Remove from heat, cover and keep warm.

3. Whisk oil, juice of 2 lime wedges, garlic and salt in small bowl until well blended.

4. Drain pasta and beans; divide between two plates. Stir oil mixture into tomato mixture; spoon over pasta and beans. Sprinkle with cilantro; serve with remaining lime wedges. *Makes 2 servings*

Tip: The remaining beans may be stored in an airtight container and frozen for up to 1 month.

Nutrients per Serving

Calories: 298, **Total Fat:** 8g, **Saturated Fat:** 1g, **Cholesterol:** 0mg, **Sodium:** 571mg, **Carbohydrate:** 50g, **Fiber:** 10g, **Protein:** 13g

lentil & orzo salad

8 cups water

½ cup uncooked dried lentils, rinsed and sorted

4 ounces uncooked orzo pasta

1½ cups quartered cherry tomatoes

¾ cup finely chopped celery

½ cup chopped red onion

2 ounces pitted olives (about 16 olives), coarsely chopped

3 to 4 tablespoons cider vinegar

1 tablespoon olive oil

1 tablespoon dried basil

1 medium clove garlic, minced

⅛ teaspoon dried red pepper flakes

4 ounces feta cheese with sun-dried tomatoes and basil

1. Bring water to boil in large saucepan or Dutch oven over high heat. Add lentils; cook 12 minutes.

2. Add pasta; cook 10 minutes or just until tender. Drain pasta and lentils; rinse under cold water to cool completely. Drain well.

3. Meanwhile, combine tomatoes, celery, onion, olives, vinegar, oil, basil, garlic and red pepper flakes in large bowl.

4. Add lentil mixture to tomato mixture; toss gently to blend. Add cheese; toss gently. Let stand 15 minutes before serving.   *Makes 4 servings*

Nutrients per Serving (1⅓ cups)

Calories: 343, **Total Fat:** 13g, **Saturated Fat:** 5g, **Cholesterol:** 21mg, **Sodium:** 470mg, **Carbohydrate:** 44g, **Fiber:** 11g, **Protein:** 17g

spaghetti with creamy tomato-pepper sauce

2 tablespoons olive oil

1 small onion, chopped

2 tablespoons minced garlic

1 large red bell pepper, chopped

2 large tomatoes, seeded and chopped (about 3 cups)

½ cup grated Parmesan cheese

¼ cup fat-free half-and-half

½ teaspoon black pepper

8 cups hot cooked multigrain or whole wheat spaghetti

1. Heat oil in large skillet over medium-low heat. Add onion and garlic; cook and stir over medium heat 5 minutes or until onion is soft. Add bell pepper; cook and stir 4 minutes or until pepper is crisp-tender. Stir in tomatoes.

2. Reduce heat to low; gradually stir in cheese, half-and-half and black pepper. Cook 5 minutes or until heated through. Serve sauce over pasta.

Makes 6 servings

Tip: To seed a tomato, cut it in half crosswise, not top to bottom. Then scrape the seeds out using a teaspoon.

Nutrients per Serving (1¼ cups)

Calories: 340, **Total Fat:** 8g, **Saturated Fat:** 2g, **Cholesterol:** 8mg, **Sodium:** 124mg, **Carbohydrate:** 58g, **Fiber:** 10g, **Protein:** 16g

main dishes

tuscan-style sausage skillet

  2 teaspoons olive oil

  ½ cup chopped fresh fennel

  ½ cup chopped sweet or yellow onion

  3 cloves garlic, minced

  1 can (about 14 ounces) fire-roasted diced tomatoes

  1 package (9 ounces) fully cooked chicken Italian sausage,*
    cut into ½-inch-thick slices

  ¾ teaspoon dried rosemary, crushed

  1 can (about 15 ounces) no-salt-added navy or Great Northern beans,
    drained

  4 cups baby spinach or torn spinach

If unavailable, use fully cooked turkey Italian sausage.

1. Heat oil in large deep skillet over medium-high heat. Add fennel, onion
and garlic; cook and stir 5 minutes.

2. Stir in tomatoes, sausage and rosemary. Reduce heat to low; cover and
simmer 10 minutes or until vegetables are tender. Stir in beans; cook over
medium-high heat until heated through.

3. Stir in spinach; cover and cook 2 minutes or until spinach wilts.

Makes 4 servings

Note: Eating spinach with meat, poultry, fish or vitamin C-rich foods
helps to enhance the absorption of iron.

Nutrients per Serving (1¼ cups)

Calories: 336, **Total Fat:** 9g, **Saturated Fat:** 2g, **Cholesterol:** 45mg,
Sodium: 708mg, **Carbohydrate:** 42g, **Fiber:** 15g, **Protein:** 24g

chili-topped baked potato

2 russet potatoes
1 tablespoon vegetable oil
2 cloves garlic, finely chopped
1½ cups thinly sliced fresh mushrooms
⅔ cup chopped red onion
⅔ cup chopped red bell pepper
¼ teaspoon ground cumin
⅛ teaspoon ground red pepper
⅛ teaspoon dried oregano
1 can (28 ounces) no-salt-added whole peeled tomatoes, undrained
½ cup canned Great Northern beans, rinsed and drained
2 green onions, sliced
¼ cup (1 ounce) shredded reduced-fat Cheddar cheese

1. Preheat oven to 450°F. Pierce potatoes several times with fork. Place in shallow baking pan; bake 45 minutes or until soft.

2. Meanwhile, heat oil in large nonstick saucepan over medium-high heat. Add garlic; cook and stir 1 minute. Add mushrooms, red onion and bell pepper; cook 5 minutes, stirring occasionally. Add cumin, ground red pepper and oregano; cook and stir 1 minute. Stir in tomatoes with juice and beans. Reduce heat to medium-low; simmer 15 minutes, stirring occasionally.

3. Cut potatoes in half lengthwise. Top with chili; sprinkle with green onions and cheese. *Makes 4 servings*

Nutrients per Serving (½ potato with 1 cup chili)

Calories: 280, **Total Fat:** 6g, **Saturated Fat:** 2g, **Cholesterol:** 5mg, **Sodium:** 230mg, **Carbohydrate:** 49g, **Fiber:** 7g, **Protein:** 11g

Chili-Topped Baked Potatoes

seasoned chicken with beans & rice

1 teaspoon vegetable oil
½ cup chopped green onions
1 teaspoon minced garlic
1½ cups fat-free reduced-sodium chicken broth
2 tablespoons all-purpose flour
3 cups frozen mixed vegetables
1 can (about 15 ounces) kidney beans, rinsed and drained
1 cup shredded cooked chicken
1 teaspoon dried rosemary
½ teaspoon dried thyme
⅛ teaspoon ground red pepper
2 cups hot cooked brown rice

1. Heat oil in large nonstick skillet over medium heat. Add green onions and garlic; cook and stir 1 minute.

2. Whisk broth and flour in medium bowl until well blended; add to skillet. Stir in frozen vegetables, beans, chicken, rosemary, thyme and red pepper; bring to a boil. Reduce heat to low; cover and simmer 6 minutes or until vegetables are tender.

3. Serve chicken and vegetables over rice.   *Makes 4 servings*

Nutrients per Serving (1½ cups)

Calories: 397, **Total Fat:** 5g, **Saturated Fat:** 1g, **Cholesterol:** 53mg, **Sodium:** 603mg, **Carbohydrate:** 58g, **Fiber:** 14g, **Protein:** 31g

Seasoned Chicken with Beans & Rice

italian eggplant with millet & pepper stuffing

¼ cup uncooked millet

2 small eggplants (about ¾ pound total)

¼ cup chopped red bell pepper, divided

¼ cup chopped green bell pepper, divided

1 teaspoon olive oil

1 clove garlic, minced

1½ cups fat-free reduced-sodium vegetable broth

½ teaspoon ground cumin

½ teaspoon dried oregano

⅛ teaspoon red pepper flakes

1. Cook and stir millet in large heavy skillet over medium heat 5 minutes or until golden. Transfer to small bowl.

2. Cut eggplants in half lengthwise. Scoop out flesh, leaving about ¼-inch-thick shell. Reserve shells; chop eggplant flesh. Combine 1 tablespoon red bell pepper and 1 teaspoon green bell pepper in small bowl; set aside.

3. Heat oil in same skillet over medium heat. Add chopped eggplant, remaining red and green bell pepper and garlic; cook and stir about 8 minutes or until eggplant is tender.

4. Stir in toasted millet, broth, cumin, oregano and red pepper flakes; bring to a boil over high heat. Reduce heat to medium-low; cover and cook 35 minutes or until liquid is absorbed and millet is tender. Remove from heat; cover and let stand 10 minutes. Preheat oven to 350°F.

5. Pour 1 cup water into 8-inch square baking pan. Fill eggplant shells with eggplant-millet mixture. Sprinkle with reserved chopped bell peppers, pressing in lightly. Carefully place filled shells in prepared pan. Bake 15 minutes or until heated through. *Makes 2 main-dish servings or 4 side-dish servings*

Nutrients per Serving (1 eggplant with stuffing)

Calories: 244, **Total Fat:** 6g, **Saturated Fat:** <1g, **Cholesterol:** 18mg, **Sodium:** 198mg, **Carbohydrate:** 40g, **Fiber:** 14g, **Protein:** 12g

tuscan turkey with white beans

1 teaspoon dried rosemary, divided

½ teaspoon garlic salt

½ teaspoon black pepper, divided

1 pound turkey breast cutlets, pounded to ¼-inch thickness

2 teaspoons canola oil, divided

1 can (about 15 ounces) no-salt-added navy beans or Great Northern beans, rinsed and drained

1 can (about 14 ounces) fire-roasted diced tomatoes

¼ cup grated Parmesan cheese

1. Combine ½ teaspoon rosemary, garlic salt and ¼ teaspoon pepper in small bowl; mix well. Sprinkle over cutlets.

2. Heat 1 teaspoon oil in large nonstick skillet over medium heat. Add half of cutlets; cook 2 to 3 minutes per side or until no longer pink in center. Transfer to serving platter; tent with foil to keep warm. Repeat with remaining oil and cutlets.

3. Add beans, tomatoes, remaining ½ teaspoon rosemary and ¼ teaspoon pepper to same skillet; bring to a boil over high heat. Reduce heat to low; simmer 5 minutes.

4. Spoon bean mixture over cutlets on serving platter; sprinkle with cheese.

Makes 6 servings

Nutrients per Serving (about 1 cup)

Calories: 230, **Total Fat:** 4g, **Saturated Fat:** 1g, **Cholesterol:** 36mg, **Sodium:** 334mg, **Carbohydrate:** 23g, **Fiber:** 9g, **Protein:** 25g

Tuscan Turkey with White Beans

beef fajitas

1 teaspoon ground cumin

1 teaspoon dried oregano

¾ pound well-trimmed boneless beef top sirloin steak (about ¾-inch thick)

2 bell peppers, cut into thin 1-inch strips

½ cup thinly sliced yellow or red onion

4 cloves garlic, minced

½ cup jalapeño salsa

4 (7-inch) high-fiber whole wheat flour tortillas, warmed

¼ cup chopped fresh cilantro

1. Rub cumin and oregano over both sides of steak. Spray large nonstick skillet with nonstick cooking spray; heat over medium heat. Add steak; cook 3 to 4 minutes per side for medium-rare doneness. Transfer steak to carving board; tent with foil and let stand.

2. Add bell peppers, onion and garlic to same skillet. Spray with nonstick cooking spray; cook and stir 4 to 5 minutes or until vegetables are crisp-tender. Stir in salsa; simmer 3 minutes.

3. Cut steak into thin slices; return to skillet. Toss with vegetables; cook about 1 minute or just until heated through.

4. Spoon mixture down center of tortillas; top with cilantro and fold in half.

Makes 4 servings

Nutrients per Serving (1 fajita)

Calories: 240, **Total Fat:** 7g, **Saturated Fat:** 2g, **Cholesterol:** 35mg, **Sodium:** 610mg, **Carbohydrate:** 28g, **Fiber:** 15g, **Protein:** 29g

quinoa with roasted vegetables

2 medium sweet potatoes, cut into ½-inch-thick slices
1 medium eggplant, peeled and cut into ½-inch cubes
1 medium tomato, cut into wedges
1 large green bell pepper, sliced
1 small onion, cut into wedges
½ teaspoon salt
¼ teaspoon black pepper
¼ teaspoon ground red pepper
1 cup uncooked quinoa
2 cloves garlic, minced
½ teaspoon dried thyme
¼ teaspoon dried marjoram
2 cups water or fat-free reduced-sodium vegetable broth

1. Preheat oven to 450°F. Line large jelly-roll pan with foil; spray with nonstick cooking spray.

2. Arrange sweet potatoes, eggplant, tomato, bell pepper and onion on prepared pan; spray lightly with cooking spray. Sprinkle with salt, black pepper and ground red pepper; toss to coat. Roast 20 to 30 minutes or until vegetables are tender and browned.

3. Meanwhile, place quinoa in strainer; rinse well. Spray medium saucepan with cooking spray; heat over medium heat. Add garlic, thyme and marjoram; cook and stir 1 to 2 minutes. Add quinoa; cook and stir 2 to 3 minutes. Stir in water; bring to a boil over high heat. Reduce heat to low; cover and simmer 15 to 20 minutes or until water is absorbed. (Quinoa will appear somewhat translucent.)

4. Transfer quinoa to large bowl; gently stir in roasted vegetables.

Makes 6 servings

Nutrients per Serving

Calories: 193, **Total Fat:** 2g, **Saturated Fat:** <1g, **Cholesterol:** 0mg, **Sodium:** 194mg, **Carbohydrate:** 40g, **Fiber:** 6g, **Protein:** 6g

Quinoa with Roasted Vegetables

polenta lasagna

4¼ cups water, divided

1½ cups whole grain yellow cornmeal

4 teaspoons finely chopped fresh marjoram

1 teaspoon olive oil

1 pound fresh mushrooms, sliced

1 cup chopped leeks

1 clove garlic, minced

½ cup (2 ounces) shredded part-skim mozzarella cheese

2 tablespoons chopped fresh basil

1 tablespoon chopped fresh oregano

⅛ teaspoon black pepper

2 medium red bell peppers, chopped

¼ cup grated Parmesan cheese, divided

1. Bring 4 cups water to a boil in medium saucepan over high heat. Slowly add cornmeal to water, stirring constantly with wire whisk. Reduce heat to low; stir in marjoram. Simmer 15 to 20 minutes or until polenta thickens and pulls away from side of saucepan. Spread in ungreased 13×9-inch baking pan. Cover and refrigerate about 1 hour or until firm.

2. Heat oil in medium nonstick skillet over medium heat. Add mushrooms, leeks and garlic; cook and stir 5 minutes or until leeks are crisp-tender. Stir in mozzarella, basil, oregano and black pepper.

3. Place bell peppers and remaining ¼ cup water in food processor or blender; process until smooth. Preheat oven to 350°F. Spray 11×7-inch baking dish with nonstick cooking spray.

4. Cut cold polenta into 12 (3½-inch) squares; arrange 6 squares in bottom of prepared dish. Spread with half of bell pepper mixture, half of vegetable mixture and 2 tablespoons Parmesan. Place remaining 6 squares polenta over Parmesan; top with remaining bell pepper and vegetable mixtures and Parmesan. Bake 20 minutes or until cheese is melted and polenta is golden brown.

Makes 6 servings

Nutrients per Serving

Calories: 195, **Total Fat:** 5g, **Saturated Fat:** 2g, **Cholesterol:** 9mg, **Sodium:** 128mg, **Carbohydrate:** 31g, **Fiber:** 4g, **Protein:** 9g

sloppy joe sliders

¾ pound 90% lean ground beef

1 can (about 14 ounces) stewed tomatoes with Mexican seasonings

½ cup frozen mixed vegetables, thawed

½ cup chopped green bell pepper

3 tablespoons ketchup

2 teaspoons Worcestershire sauce

1 teaspoon ground cumin

1 teaspoon cider vinegar

24 mini (1 ounce each) whole wheat rolls, split and warmed

1. Cook ground beef in large nonstick skillet over medium-high heat 6 to 8 minutes or until browned, stirring to break up meat.

2. Add tomatoes, mixed vegetables, bell pepper, ketchup, Worcestershire sauce, cumin and vinegar; bring to a boil. Reduce heat to low; cover and simmer 15 minutes or until peppers are tender and mixture has thickened. Break up large pieces of tomato.

3. Spoon 2 tablespoons beef mixture on each roll.   *Makes 24 sliders*

Nutrients per Serving (3 sliders)

Calories: 324, **Total Fat:** 7g, **Saturated Fat:** 2g, **Cholesterol:** 23mg, **Sodium:** 620mg, **Carbohydrate:** 50g, **Fiber:** 8g, **Protein:** 17g

barley & swiss chard skillet

1 cup water
1 cup chopped red bell pepper
1 cup chopped green bell pepper
¾ cup quick-cooking barley
⅛ teaspoon garlic powder
⅛ teaspoon red pepper flakes
2 cups packed coarsely chopped Swiss chard*
1 cup canned reduced-sodium navy beans, rinsed and drained
1 cup quartered cherry tomatoes
¼ cup chopped fresh basil leaves
1 tablespoon olive oil
2 tablespoons Italian-seasoned dry bread crumbs

Fresh spinach or beet greens can be substituted for Swiss chard.

1. Preheat broiler.

2. Bring water to a boil in large ovenproof skillet; add bell peppers, barley, garlic powder and red pepper flakes. Reduce heat to low; cover and simmer 10 minutes or until liquid is absorbed. Remove from heat.

3. Stir in chard, beans, tomatoes, basil and oil. Sprinkle with bread crumbs. Broil 2 minutes or until golden.

Makes 4 servings

Nutrients per Serving (1¼ cups)

Calories: 288, **Total Fat:** 6g, **Saturated Fat:** <1g, **Cholesterol:** 0mg, **Sodium:** 488mg, **Carbohydrate:** 45g, **Fiber:** 12g, **Protein:** 10g

chunky italian stew with white beans

1 teaspoon olive oil
2 green bell peppers, cut into ¾-inch pieces
1 yellow squash, cut into ¾-inch pieces
1 zucchini, cut into ¾-inch pieces
1 onion, cut into ¾-inch pieces
4 ounces mushrooms, quartered (about 1 cup)
1 can (about 15 ounces) reduced-sodium navy beans, rinsed and drained
1 can (about 14 ounces) reduced-sodium diced tomatoes
1 teaspoon dried oregano
½ teaspoon sugar
½ teaspoon Italian seasoning
⅛ teaspoon red pepper flakes (optional)
¾ cup (3 ounces) shredded part-skim mozzarella cheese
1 tablespoon grated Parmesan cheese

1. Heat oil in large saucepan or Dutch oven over medium-high heat. Add bell peppers, squash, zucchini, onion and mushrooms; cook and stir 8 minutes or until onion is translucent.

2. Stir in beans, tomatoes, oregano, sugar, Italian seasoning and red pepper flakes, if desired. Reduce heat to low; cover and simmer 15 minutes or until vegetables are tender, stirring once.

3. Sprinkle with cheeses just before serving.

Makes 4 servings

Nutrients per Serving (1½ cups)

Calories: 265, **Total Fat:** 6g, **Saturated Fat:** 3g, **Cholesterol:** 15mg, **Sodium:** 208mg, **Carbohydrate:** 38g, **Fiber:** 9g, **Protein:** 17g

Chunky Italian Stew with White Beans

middle eastern grilled vegetable wraps

1 large eggplant (about 1 pound), cut crosswise into ⅜-inch slices
¾ pound large fresh mushrooms
1 medium red bell pepper, cut into quarters
1 medium green bell pepper, cut into quarters
2 green onions, sliced
¼ cup fresh lemon juice
⅛ teaspoon black pepper
4 large (10-inch) fat-free flour tortillas
½ cup (4 ounces) hummus
⅓ cup lightly packed fresh cilantro
12 large fresh basil leaves
12 large fresh mint leaves
2 tablespoons finely chopped red and/or green bell pepper (optional)

1. Prepare grill for direct cooking.

2. Lightly spray eggplant slices with nonstick cooking spray. Thread any small mushrooms onto metal skewers.

3. Grill bell peppers, skin side down, over hot coals until skins are blackened. Place in paper bag; close bag. Let stand 5 to 10 minutes or until cool enough to handle. Peel peppers. Grill eggplant and mushrooms, covered, over medium coals about 2 minutes per side or until tender and lightly browned.

4. Cut eggplant and bell peppers into ½-inch strips; cut mushrooms into quarters. Combine vegetables, green onions, lemon juice and black pepper in medium bowl.

5. Grill tortillas about 1 minute or until warm, turning once. Spoon 2 tablespoons hummus down center of each tortilla. Top with one quarter of cilantro, 3 basil leaves, 3 mint leaves and one quarter of vegetables. Roll up tortillas to enclose filling. Serve immediately. Garnish with chopped bell pepper. *Makes 4 servings*

Nutrients per Serving (1 wrap)

Calories: 234, **Total Fat:** 6g, **Saturated Fat:** 1g, **Cholesterol:** 0mg,
Sodium: 340mg, **Carbohydrate:** 41g, **Fiber:** 14g, **Protein:** 8g

Middle Eastern Grilled Vegetable Wrap

rosemary-garlic scallops with polenta

2 teaspoons olive oil

1 medium red bell pepper, cut into strips

⅓ cup chopped red onion

3 cloves garlic, minced

½ pound fresh bay scallops

2 teaspoons chopped fresh rosemary *or* ¾ teaspoon dried rosemary

¼ teaspoon black pepper

1¼ cups fat-free reduced-sodium chicken broth

½ cup cornmeal

¼ teaspoon salt

1. Heat oil in large nonstick skillet over medium heat. Add bell pepper, onion and garlic; cook and stir 5 minutes. Add scallops, rosemary and black pepper; cook 3 to 5 minutes or until scallops are opaque, stirring occasionally.

2. Meanwhile, combine broth, cornmeal and salt in small saucepan; bring to a boil over high heat. Reduce heat to low; simmer 5 minutes or until polenta is very thick, stirring frequently.

3. Spoon polenta onto two serving plates; top with scallop mixture.

Makes 2 servings

Nutrients per Serving (1¾ cups)

Calories: 304, **Total Fat:** 8g, **Saturated Fat:** 1g, **Cholesterol:** 53mg, **Sodium:** 731mg, **Carbohydrate:** 33g, **Fiber:** 4g, **Protein:** 26g

There are two common varieties of scallops: bay and sea. Bay scallops are smaller and usually average about 100 per pound. Sea scallops are much larger, averaging about 30 per pound. Sea scallops cut into halves or thirds can easily substitute for bay scallops if the latter are not available.

Rosemary-Garlic Scallops with Polenta

chickpea burgers

1 can (about 15 ounces) chickpeas, rinsed and drained
⅓ cup chopped carrots
⅓ cup herbed croutons
¼ cup chopped fresh parsley
¼ cup chopped onion
1 egg white
1 teaspoon minced garlic
1 teaspoon grated lemon peel
½ teaspoon black pepper
⅛ teaspoon salt (optional)
4 whole grain hamburger buns
   Tomato slices, lettuce leaves and salsa (optional)

1. Place chickpeas, carrots, croutons, parsley, onion, egg white, garlic, lemon peel, pepper and salt, if desired, in food processor; process until blended. Shape mixture into 4 patties.

2. Spray large nonstick skillet with nonstick cooking spray; heat over medium heat. Cook patties 4 to 5 minutes or until bottoms are browned. Spray tops of patties with cooking spray; turn and cook 4 to 5 minutes or until browned.

3. Serve burgers on buns with tomato, lettuce and salsa, if desired.

Makes 4 servings

Nutrients per Serving (1 burger)

Calories: 271, **Total Fat:** 5g, **Saturated Fat:** <1g, **Cholesterol:** <1mg, **Sodium:** 272mg, **Carbohydrate:** 48g, **Fiber:** 7g, **Protein:** 11g

Chickpea Burger

sausage, barley & spinach stuffed mushrooms

½ cup quick-cooking barley

1 cup reduced-sodium chicken broth

2 links (8 ounces) hot or mild turkey Italian sausage*

3 cups packed baby spinach leaves

4 large portobello mushroom caps, stems removed

Olive oil cooking spray

¼ cup crumbled blue cheese

Or substitute turkey breakfast sausage links.

1. Preheat oven to 450°F. Combine barley and broth in medium saucepan; bring to a boil over high heat. Reduce heat to low; cover and simmer 12 to 14 minutes or until barley is tender and liquid is absorbed.

2. Meanwhile, remove sausage from casings; cook in large nonstick skillet over medium-high heat until no longer pink, stirring to break up meat. Drain fat. Add spinach, stirring until wilted. Combine sausage mixture and barley; mix well.

3. Line baking sheet with foil; spray with cooking spray. Remove and discard gills from undersides of mushroom caps. Place caps, rounded sides up, on prepared baking sheet; spray tops lightly with cooking spray.

4. Bake 5 minutes or until hot. Turn mushroom caps; spoon barley mixture evenly into caps and top with cheese. Bake 6 to 8 minutes or until mushrooms are tender and stuffing is heated through. *Makes 4 servings*

Note: Barley is a whole grain rich in both soluble and insoluble fiber. It also contains vitamins, minerals, antioxidants and phytochemicals.

Nutrients per Serving (1 mushroom cap with stuffing)

Calories: 234, **Total Fat:** 8g, **Saturated Fat:** 3g, **Cholesterol:** 43mg, **Sodium:** 490mg, **Carbohydrate:** 26g, **Fiber:** 5g, **Protein:** 18g

broccoli slaw with chicken & honey-lime dressing

¼ cup fresh lime juice
1½ tablespoons olive oil
2 tablespoons seasoned rice wine vinegar
2 teaspoons honey
1 teaspoon cumin
1 small clove garlic, crushed
¼ teaspoon salt
¼ teaspoon black pepper
2 packages (9 ounces each) broccoli coleslaw
2 cups shredded cooked chicken
1 cup black beans, drained and rinsed
½ cup thinly sliced green onion

1. Whisk lime juice, oil, vinegar, honey, cumin, garlic, salt and pepper in small bowl until well blended.

2. Place broccoli slaw, chicken, beans and green onion in large bowl; toss gently.

3. Drizzle dressing over slaw; toss gently to coat. Refrigerate at least 1 hour to let flavors blend. Toss again before serving.   *Makes 4 servings*

Nutrients per Serving (2 cups salad with 2 tablespoons dressing)

Calories: 272, **Total Fat:** 10g, **Saturated Fat:** 2g, **Cholesterol:** 58mg, **Sodium:** 555mg, **Carbohydrate:** 24g, **Fiber:** 7g, **Protein:** 26g

vegetable risotto

2 tablespoons olive oil, divided
1 medium zucchini, cubed
1 medium yellow squash, cubed
1 cup sliced, stemmed shiitake mushrooms
1 cup chopped onion
1 clove garlic, minced
3 plum tomatoes, seeded and chopped
1 teaspoon dried oregano
3 cups vegetable broth
1 cup uncooked arborio rice
¼ cup grated Parmesan cheese
    Salt and black pepper (optional)
½ cup frozen peas, thawed

1. Heat 1 tablespoon oil in large saucepan over medium heat. Add zucchini and yellow squash; cook and stir 5 minutes or until crisp-tender. Transfer to medium bowl.

2. Add mushrooms, onion and garlic to saucepan; cook and stir 5 minutes or until tender. Add tomatoes and oregano; cook and stir 2 to 3 minutes or until tomatoes soften. Transfer to bowl with zucchini mixture. Heat broth to a simmer in small saucepan over medium-low heat; keep warm.

3. Meanwhile, heat remaining 1 tablespoon oil in large saucepan over medium heat. Add rice; cook and stir 2 minutes.

4. Stir about ¾ cup broth into rice; cook and stir until broth is absorbed. Repeat with remaining broth, adding ¾ cup at a time, stirring constantly until broth is absorbed before adding next ¾ cup. Cook until rice is tender but not mushy. (Total cooking time will be 20 to 25 minutes.)

5. Stir in cheese; season to taste with salt and pepper, if desired. Stir in reserved vegetables and peas; cook until heated through. Serve immediately.

Makes 4 to 6 servings

Nutrients per Serving

Calories: 394, **Total Fat:** 9g, **Saturated Fat:** 2g, **Cholesterol:** 4mg, **Sodium:** 519mg, **Carbohydrate:** 56g, **Fiber:** 5g, **Protein:** 10g

Vegetable Risotto

lemon shrimp with black beans & rice

1 cup uncooked instant brown rice

⅛ teaspoon ground turmeric

1 pound raw shrimp, peeled and deveined (with tails on)

1½ teaspoons chili powder

½ (15-ounce) can reduced-sodium black beans, rinsed and drained

1 medium poblano pepper *or* ½ green bell pepper, minced

1½ to 2 teaspoons grated lemon peel

3 tablespoons lemon juice

1½ tablespoons extra virgin olive oil

⅛ teaspoon salt

Lemon wedges (optional)

1. Cook rice with turmeric according to package directions, omitting salt and fat.

2. Spray large nonstick skillet with nonstick cooking spray; heat over medium heat. Add shrimp and chili powder; cook and stir 4 minutes or until shrimp are pink and opaque. Add beans, pepper, lemon peel, lemon juice, oil and salt; cook and stir 1 minute or until heated through.

3. Spoon shrimp mixture over rice. Garnish with lemon wedges.

Makes 4 servings

Nutrients per Serving (1½ cups)

Calories: 306, **Total Fat:** 8g, **Saturated Fat:** 1g, **Cholesterol:** 172mg, **Sodium:** 371mg, **Carbohydrate:** 33g, **Fiber:** 4g, **Protein:** 28g

Lemon Shrimp with Black Beans & Rice

broccoli pescetore

1 jar (26 ounces) reduced-sodium marinara pasta sauce

1 can (about 15 ounces) reduced-sodium white beans, rinsed and drained

1 can (6 ounces) tuna packed in water, drained

1 tablespoon chopped or minced garlic

2 teaspoons dried oregano

1 bag (12 ounces) ready-to-use broccoli florets

¼ cup grated Parmesan cheese

Black pepper (optional)

1. Combine pasta sauce, beans, tuna, garlic and oregano in medium saucepan. Cook over medium-high heat about 6 minutes or until heated through.

2. Prepare broccoli florets according to package directions. Divide broccoli between four pasta bowls. Spoon sauce evenly over broccoli; sprinkle with cheese and pepper, if desired. *Makes 4 servings*

Nutrients per Serving

Calories: 373, **Total Fat:** 9g, **Saturated Fat:** 2g, **Cholesterol:** 17mg, **Sodium:** 822mg, **Carbohydrate:** 47g, **Fiber:** 17g, **Protein:** 27g

Tuna is a nutrient-dense food—a great source of protein, essential vitamins and minerals, and omega-3 fatty acids. It is very low in saturated fat, sodium and cholesterol, and it contains no carbohydrates.

jamaican black bean stew

2 cups uncooked brown rice

2 pounds sweet potatoes

3 pounds butternut squash

1 can (about 14 ounces) vegetable broth

1 large onion, coarsely chopped

3 cloves garlic, minced

1 tablespoon curry powder

1½ teaspoons ground allspice

½ teaspoon ground red pepper

¼ teaspoon salt

2 cans (about 15 ounces each) black beans, rinsed and drained

½ cup raisins

3 tablespoons fresh lime juice

1 cup diced tomato

1 cup diced peeled cucumber

1. Prepare rice according to package directions. Meanwhile, peel sweet potatoes; cut into ¾-inch chunks to measure 4 cups. Peel squash and remove seeds; cut into ¾-inch cubes to measure 5 cups.

2. Combine sweet potatoes, squash, broth, onion, garlic, curry powder, allspice, red pepper and salt in Dutch oven; bring to a boil over high heat. Reduce heat to low; cover and simmer 15 minutes or until sweet potatoes and squash are tender.

3. Add beans and raisins; simmer 5 minutes or until heated through. Stir in lime juice. Serve stew over brown rice; top with tomato and cucumber.

Makes 8 servings

Nutrients per Serving

Calories: 463, **Total Fat:** 4g, **Saturated Fat:** 1g, **Cholesterol:** 0mg, **Sodium:** 439mg, **Carbohydrate:** 102g, **Fiber:** 10g, **Protein:** 16g

chickpea vegetable curry

2 teaspoons canola or vegetable oil

4 cups cut fresh vegetables such as bell peppers, broccoli, celery, carrots, zucchini and red onion

3 cloves garlic, minced

2 cups low-sodium vegetable broth, divided

1½ teaspoons curry powder

¼ teaspoon ground red pepper

1 can (about 15 ounces) no-salt-added chickpeas, undrained

⅓ cup golden raisins

¼ to ½ teaspoon salt (optional)

¾ cup uncooked whole wheat couscous

¼ cup chopped fresh cilantro

¼ cup sliced almonds, toasted (optional)

1. Heat oil in large saucepan over medium heat. Add vegetables; cook 5 minutes, stirring occasionally. Add garlic; cook and stir 1 minute. Stir in 1 cup broth, curry powder and red pepper; bring to a boil. Reduce heat to low; cover and simmer 6 minutes. Stir in chickpeas, raisins and salt, if desired; cover and simmer 2 to 3 minutes or until vegetables are tender.

2. Meanwhile, bring remaining 1 cup broth to a boil in small saucepan over medium-high heat. Stir in couscous. Remove from heat; cover and let stand 5 minutes.

3. Stir in cilantro and almonds, if desired, with fork. Spoon couscous mixture into bowls; top with curry mixture.   *Makes 4 servings*

Tip: To toast almonds, spread them in a small nonstick skillet; cook and stir over medium heat until lightly browned. Remove them to a plate to cool.

Nutrients per Serving (1¼ cups curry with ½ cup couscous)

Calories: 291, **Total Fat:** 5g, **Saturated Fat:** <1g, **Cholesterol:** 0mg, **Sodium:** 113mg, **Carbohydrate:** 51g, **Fiber:** 12g, **Protein:** 14g

salads & sides

tuna tabouleh salad

 1 cup water
¾ cup uncooked fine-grain bulgur wheat
 1 teaspoon grated lemon peel
 3 tablespoons lemon juice
 1 small clove garlic, minced
½ teaspoon salt
⅛ teaspoon black pepper
 1 tablespoon olive oil
 1 cup red or yellow cherry tomatoes, quartered if large
 1 cup chopped cucumber
¼ cup finely chopped red onion
 3 cans (5 ounces each) chunk white albacore tuna packed in water,
    drained and flaked
½ cup chopped Italian parsley
 4 cups watercress, tough stems removed

1. Bring water to a boil in small saucepan. Remove from heat and add bulgur; cover and let stand 15 minutes. Place bulgur in fine mesh sieve; run under cold water to cool. Drain well.

2. Meanwhile, whisk lemon peel, lemon juice, garlic, salt and pepper in large bowl. Slowly whisk in olive oil. Add tomatoes, cucumber, onion and bulgur; stir to combine. Gently stir in tuna and parsley.

3. Arrange watercress on 4 serving plates; spoon about 1½ cups salad onto each plate.   *Makes 4 servings*

Nutrients per Serving (1½ cups)

Calories: 282, **Total Fat:** 8g, **Saturated Fat:** 1g, **Cholesterol:** 45mg, **Sodium:** 365mg, **Carbohydrate:** 22g, **Fiber:** 4g, **Protein:** 31g

garden potato salad with basil-yogurt dressing

    3 cups water
    6 new potatoes, quartered
    8 ounces asparagus, cut into 1-inch slices
 1¼ cups bell pepper strips
  ⅔ cup plain low-fat yogurt
  ¼ cup sliced green onions
    2 tablespoons chopped pitted ripe olives
 1½ tablespoons chopped fresh basil *or* 1½ teaspoons dried basil
    1 tablespoon chopped fresh thyme *or* 1 teaspoon dried thyme
    1 tablespoon white vinegar
    2 teaspoons sugar
      Dash ground red pepper

1. Bring water to a boil in large saucepan over high heat. Add potatoes; return to a boil. Reduce heat to medium-low; cover and simmer 8 minutes.

2. Add asparagus and bell peppers to saucepan; return to a boil over high heat. Reduce heat to medium-low; cover and simmer about 3 minutes or until potatoes are just tender and asparagus and bell peppers are crisp-tender. Drain.

3. Meanwhile, combine yogurt, green onions, olives, basil, thyme, vinegar, sugar and ground red pepper in large bowl. Add vegetables; toss to coat. Cover and refrigerate until well chilled.   *Makes 4 servings*

Nutrients per Serving

Calories: 154, **Total Fat:** 3g, **Saturated Fat:** 1g, **Cholesterol:** 2mg, **Sodium:** 173mg, **Carbohydrate:** 30g, **Fiber:** 3g, **Protein:** 6g

Garden Potato Salad with Basil-Yogurt Dressing

chicken & couscous salad

1 can (about 14 ounces) fat-free reduced-sodium chicken broth
½ teaspoon ground cinnamon
¼ teaspoon ground nutmeg
¼ teaspoon curry powder
1 cup uncooked couscous
1½ pounds boneless skinless chicken breasts, cooked and cut into 1-inch pieces
2 cups fresh pineapple chunks
2 cups cubed seeded cucumber chunks
2 cups cubed red bell pepper
2 cups cubed yellow bell pepper
1 cup sliced celery
½ cup sliced green onions with tops
3 tablespoons water
3 tablespoons apple cider vinegar
2 tablespoons vegetable oil
1 tablespoon fresh mint *or* 1 teaspoon dried mint

1. Combine broth, cinnamon, nutmeg and curry powder in large nonstick saucepan; bring to a boil. Stir in couscous. Remove from heat; cover and let stand 5 minutes. Fluff couscous with fork; transfer to serving bowl. Cool to room temperature.

2. Add chicken, pineapple, cucumber, bell peppers, celery and green onions to couscous; mix well.

3. Combine water, vinegar, oil and mint in small jar with tight-fitting lid; shake well. Pour dressing over couscous mixture; toss to coat. Serve immediately.

Makes 6 servings

Nutrients per Serving

Calories: 348, **Total Fat:** 8g, **Saturated Fat:** 1g, **Cholesterol:** 58mg, **Sodium:** 85mg, **Carbohydrate:** 43g, **Fiber:** 9g, **Protein:** 27g

cranberry-ginger glazed sweet potatoes

2 medium sweet potatoes
½ cup dried cranberries
¼ cup cranberry juice
¼ cup maple syrup
2 slices (⅛ inch thick) fresh ginger
Dash black pepper

Pierce potatoes with fork. Microwave on HIGH 10 minutes or until soft. Peel and cut potatoes into wedges; place in serving dish. Meanwhile, place cranberries, juice, syrup, ginger and pepper in small saucepan. Cook over low heat 7 to 10 minutes or until syrupy. Discard ginger. Pour glaze over potatoes; toss to coat.   *Makes 4 servings*

Nutrients per Serving (½ cup)

Calories: 217, **Total Fat: Saturated Fat:** <1g, **Cholesterol:** 0mg, **Sodium:** 15mg, **Carbohydrate:** 53g, **Fiber:** 4g, **Protein:** 2g

corn & roasted red pepper rice salad

2 tablespoons plus 1 teaspoon canola or vegetable oil, divided
3 cloves garlic, minced
½ cup roasted red peppers in water, drained and chopped
1 package (10 ounces) frozen corn, thawed
2 cups cooked brown rice
¼ cup chopped fresh cilantro
¼ cup fresh lime juice
1 tablespoon cumin

Heat 1 teaspoon oil in large skillet over medium heat. Add garlic; cook and stir 1 minute. Add peppers and corn; cook 2 minutes. Transfer to large bowl; stir in rice and cilantro. Whisk lime juice, remaining 2 tablespoons oil and cumin in small bowl. Add to salad; toss to coat. Refrigerate 1 hour before serving.   *Makes 4 servings*

Nutrients per Serving (¾ cup)

Calories: 233, **Total Fat:** 9g, **Saturated Fat:** <1g, **Cholesterol:** 0mg, **Sodium:** 52mg, **Carbohydrate:** 35g, **Fiber:** 4g, **Protein:** 6g

Cranberry-Ginger Glazed Sweet Potatoes

skillet succotash

 1 teaspoon canola oil
½ cup diced onion
½ cup diced green bell pepper
½ cup diced celery
½ teaspoon paprika
¾ cup frozen white or yellow corn
¾ cup frozen lima beans
½ cup canned low-sodium diced tomatoes
 1 tablespoon minced fresh parsley *or* 1 teaspoon dried parsley flakes
¼ teaspoon salt
¼ teaspoon black pepper

1. Heat oil in large skillet over medium heat. Add onion, bell pepper and celery; cook and stir 5 minutes or until onion is translucent and pepper and celery are crisp-tender. Stir in paprika.

2. Stir in corn, lima beans and tomatoes. Reduce heat to low; cover and simmer about 20 minutes or until beans are tender. Add water, 1 tablespoon at a time, if needed during cooking. Stir in parsley, salt and pepper.   *Makes 4 servings*

Tip: For additional flavor, add 1 clove minced garlic and 1 bay leaf to the skillet with the onion. Remove and discard the bay leaf before serving.

Nutrients per Serving (½ cup)

Calories: 99, **Total Fat:** 2g, **Saturated Fat:** <1g, **Cholesterol:** 0mg, **Sodium:** 187mg, **Carbohydrate:** 19g, **Fiber:** 4g, **Protein:** 4g

6-bean party salad

2 romaine lettuce hearts
1 can (about 8 ounces) reduced-sodium lima beans, rinsed and drained
1 can (about 15 ounces) reduced-sodium pinto beans, rinsed and drained
1 can (about 15 ounces) reduced-sodium red kidney beans, rinsed and drained
1 can (about 15 ounces) reduced-sodium chickpeas, rinsed and drained
1 can (about 15 ounces) reduced-sodium black beans, rinsed and drained
1 can (about 15 ounces) reduced-sodium pigeon peas, rinsed and drained
½ cup reduced-fat Italian salad dressing

1. Set aside 10 lettuce leaves for garnish. Thinly slice remaining lettuce leaves; place in large bowl.

2. Add beans and dressing to lettuce; toss gently to coat. Stand lettuce leaf upright in each of 10 glasses. Spoon 1 cup salad into each glass.   *Makes 10 servings*

Nutrients per Serving (1 cup)

Calories: 224, **Total Fat:** 2g, **Saturated Fat:** <2g, **Cholesterol:** <1mg, **Sodium:** 392mg, **Carbohydrate:** 40g, **Fiber:** 11g, **Protein:** 13g

sweet potato fries

1 large sweet potato (about 8 ounces), peeled and cut into long spears
2 teaspoons olive oil
¼ teaspoon salt (kosher or sea salt preferred)
¼ teaspoon black pepper
¼ teaspoon ground red pepper

1. Preheat oven to 350°F. Lightly spray baking sheet with cooking spray. Combine sweet potato, oil, salt, black pepper and ground red pepper on prepared baking sheet; toss to coat. Arrange potatoes in single layer (pieces should not touch).

2. Bake 45 minutes or until lightly browned.   *Makes 2 servings*

Nutrients per Serving

Calories: 139, **Total Fat:** 5g, **Saturated Fat:** <1g, **Cholesterol:** 0mg, **Sodium:** 301mg, **Carbohydrate:** 23g, **Fiber:** 4g, **Protein:** 2g

6-Bean Party Salad

barley, hazelnut & pear stuffing

3 to 3¼ cups vegetable broth, divided
½ teaspoon salt, divided
1 cup uncooked pearl barley
2 tablespoons unsalted butter, divided
1 small onion, chopped
1 stalk celery, chopped
1 large ripe Anjou pear, cut into ½-inch pieces
⅛ teaspoon black pepper
½ cup chopped toasted hazelnuts (see tip)

1. Bring 3 cups broth and ¼ teaspoon salt to a boil in large saucepan over high heat. Stir in barley. Reduce heat to low; simmer 45 minutes or until barley is tender.

2. Melt 1 tablespoon butter in large skillet over medium heat. Add onion and celery; cook and stir 5 minutes. Add remaining 1 tablespoon butter and pear; cook and stir 5 minutes.

3. Stir in barley, remaining ¼ teaspoon salt and pepper. If mixture is dry, add remaining ¼ cup broth. Stir in hazelnuts.   *Makes 6 to 8 servings*

Serving Suggestion: Spoon stuffing mixture into baked acorn or butternut squash halves. Place stuffed squash in preheated 325°F oven; bake 15 to 20 minutes or until heated through.

Tip: To toast hazelnuts, preheat oven to 325°F. Spread hazelnuts on baking sheet; bake 5 to 7 minutes. Place nuts in a kitchen towel and rub to remove skins. Coarsely chop as needed.

Nutrients per Serving

Calories: 247, **Total Fat:** 11g, **Saturated Fat:** 3g, **Cholesterol:** 11mg, **Sodium:** 684mg, **Carbohydrate:** 34g, **Fiber:** 7g, **Protein:** 6g

barley & vegetable risotto

4½ cups fat-free reduced-sodium vegetable or chicken broth
2 teaspoons olive oil
1 small onion, diced
8 ounces sliced mushrooms
¾ cup uncooked pearl barley
1 large red bell pepper, diced
2 cups packed baby spinach
¼ cup grated Parmesan cheese
¼ teaspoon black pepper

1. Heat broth to a simmer in medium saucepan over medium-low heat; keep warm.

2. Meanwhile, heat oil in large saucepan over medium heat. Add onion; cook and stir 4 minutes. Add mushrooms; cook and stir over medium-high heat 5 minutes or until mushrooms begin to brown and liquid evaporates.

3. Add barley; cook and stir 1 minute. Add ¼ cup hot broth; cook and stir about 2 minutes or until broth is almost completely absorbed. Continue adding broth, ¼ cup at a time, stirring constantly until broth is almost absorbed before adding next ¼ cup. After 20 minutes of cooking, stir in bell pepper. Continue cooking and adding broth until barley is tender. (Total cooking time will be about 30 minutes.)

4. Add spinach; cook and stir 1 minute or just until spinach is wilted. Stir in cheese and black pepper.   *Makes 6 servings*

Nutrients per Serving (½ cup)

Calories: 70, **Total Fat:** 3g, **Saturated Fat:** 1g, **Cholesterol:** 5mg, **Sodium:** 340mg, **Carbohydrate:** 7g, **Fiber:** 2g, **Protein:** 3g

spicy chickpeas & couscous

1 can (about 14 ounces) vegetable broth
1 teaspoon ground coriander
½ teaspoon ground cardamom
½ teaspoon turmeric
½ teaspoon hot pepper sauce
¼ teaspoon salt
⅛ teaspoon ground cinnamon
1 cup matchstick-size carrots
1 can (about 15 ounces) chickpeas, rinsed and drained
1 cup frozen green peas
1 cup quick-cooking couscous
2 tablespoons chopped fresh mint or parsley

1. Combine broth, coriander, cardamom, turmeric, pepper sauce, salt and cinnamon in large saucepan; bring to a boil over high heat.

2. Add carrots to saucepan; reduce heat to medium-low and simmer 5 minutes. Add chickpeas and green peas; simmer 2 minutes.

3. Stir in couscous. Remove from heat; cover and let stand 5 minutes or until liquid is absorbed. Sprinkle with mint. *Makes 6 servings*

Nutrients per Serving

Calories: 226, **Total Fat:** 2g, **Saturated Fat:** <1g, **Cholesterol:** 0mg, **Sodium:** 431mg, **Carbohydrate:** 44g, **Fiber:** 10g, **Protein:** 9g

hot three-bean casserole

2 tablespoons olive oil
1 cup coarsely chopped onion
1 cup chopped celery
2 cloves garlic, minced
1 can (about 15 ounces) chickpeas, rinsed and drained
1 can (about 15 ounces) kidney beans, rinsed and drained
1 cup coarsely chopped tomato
1 cup water
1 can (about 8 ounces) tomato sauce
1 to 2 jalapeño peppers,* minced
1 tablespoon chili powder
2 teaspoons sugar
1½ teaspoons ground cumin
1 teaspoon salt
1 teaspoon dried oregano
¼ teaspoon black pepper
2½ cups (10 ounces) frozen cut green beans
Fresh oregano (optional)

Jalapeño peppers can sting and irritate the skin, so wear rubber gloves when handling peppers and do not touch your eyes.

1. Heat oil in large skillet over medium heat. Add onion, celery and garlic; cook and stir 5 minutes or until tender.

2. Add chickpeas, kidney beans, tomato, water, tomato sauce, jalapeño, chili powder, sugar, cumin, salt, dried oregano and black pepper; bring to a boil. Reduce heat to low; simmer 20 minutes.

3. Add green beans; simmer 10 minutes or until tender. Garnish with fresh oregano.

Makes 12 servings

Nutrients per Serving (½ cup)

Calories: 118, **Total Fat:** 3g, **Saturated Fat:** <1g, **Cholesterol:** 0mg, **Sodium:** 521mg, **Carbohydrate:** 20g, **Fiber:** 6g, **Protein:** 6g

spiced rice & carrot salad

⅔ cup cooked brown rice, chilled
2 medium carrots, shredded
1 green onion, chopped
1 teaspoon white wine vinegar
1 teaspoon canola oil
1 teaspoon Chinese chili-garlic sauce
⅛ teaspoon salt
⅛ teaspoon black pepper

Combine rice, carrots and green onion in medium bowl. Whisk vinegar, oil, chili-garlic sauce, salt and pepper in small bowl until well blended. Pour dressing over rice mixture; toss to coat. *Makes 2 servings*

Nutrients per Serving (¾ cup)

Calories: 275, **Total Fat:** 4g, **Saturated Fat:** <1g, **Cholesterol:** 0mg, **Sodium:** 236mg, **Carbohydrate:** 55g, **Fiber:** 5g, **Protein:** 6g

roasted butternut squash

1 pound butternut squash, peeled and cut into 1-inch cubes (about 4 cups)
2 medium onions, coarsely chopped
8 ounces carrots, peeled and cut into ½-inch diagonal slices (about 2 cups)
1 tablespoon dark brown sugar
¼ teaspoon salt
   Black pepper (optional)
1 tablespoon butter or margarine, melted

1. Preheat oven to 400°F. Line large baking sheet with foil; spray with nonstick cooking spray. Arrange vegetables in single layer on prepared baking sheet; spray lightly with cooking spray. Sprinkle vegetables with brown sugar, salt and pepper, if desired.

2. Roast 30 minutes. Stir gently; roast 10 to 15 minutes more or until vegetables are tender. Drizzle with butter; toss to coat. *Makes 5 servings*

Nutrients per Serving (1 cup)

Calories: 143, **Total Fat:** 3g, **Saturated Fat:** 2g, **Cholesterol:** 7mg, **Sodium:** 167mg, **Carbohydrate:** 30g, **Fiber:** 8g, **Protein:** 3g

mediterranean barley-bean salad

⅔ cup uncooked pearl barley

3 cups asparagus pieces

2 cans (about 15 ounces each) dark red kidney beans, rinsed and drained

2 tablespoons chopped fresh mint

¼ cup lemon juice

¼ cup fat-free Italian salad dressing

¼ teaspoon black pepper

¼ cup dry-roasted unsalted sunflower seeds

1. Cook barley according to package directions, omitting salt and fat. Add asparagus during last 5 minutes of cooking; drain. Transfer to large bowl; refrigerate at least 2 hours.

2. Stir beans and mint into barley mixture. Whisk lemon juice, dressing and pepper in small bowl until well blended. Add to barley mixture; toss to coat. Sprinkle with sunflower seeds.

Makes 4 servings

Nutrients per Serving (scant 2 cups)

Calories: 377, **Total Fat:** 5g, **Saturated Fat:** 1g, **Cholesterol:** 0mg, **Sodium:** 946mg, **Carbohydrate:** 68g, **Fiber:** 22g, **Protein:** 18g

There are several types of barley available, typically found in supermarkets near the rice and beans. Pearl barley refers to barley that has the outer hull and some of the outer bran removed, which gives it a more uniform shape and polished appearance. It has less fiber than hulled barley, but it still packs a good nutritional punch.

bulgur pilaf with tomatoes & zucchini

1 cup uncooked bulgur wheat

1 tablespoon olive oil

¾ cup chopped onion

2 cloves garlic, minced

1 can (about 14 ounces) no-salt-added whole tomatoes, drained and coarsely chopped

½ pound zucchini (2 small), thinly sliced

1 cup fat-free reduced-sodium vegetable or chicken broth

1 teaspoon dried basil

⅛ teaspoon black pepper

1. Rinse bulgur thoroughly under cold water, removing any debris. Drain well.

2. Heat oil in large saucepan over medium heat. Add onion and garlic; cook and stir 3 minutes or until onion is tender. Stir in tomatoes and zucchini. Reduce heat to medium-low; cover and cook 15 minutes or until zucchini is almost tender, stirring occasionally.

3. Stir bulgur, broth, basil and pepper into vegetable mixture; bring to a boil over high heat. Remove from heat; cover and let stand 10 minutes or until liquid is absorbed. Stir gently before serving.   *Makes 8 servings*

Nutrients per Serving

Calories: 98, **Total Fat:** 2g, **Saturated Fat:** <1g, **Cholesterol:** 0mg, **Sodium:** 92mg, **Carbohydrate:** 18g, **Fiber:** 5g, **Protein:** 3g

desserts & snacks

cherry parfait crunch

¾ pound dark or light sweet cherries
½ cup unsweetened apple juice
¼ teaspoon ground cinnamon
   Dash ground nutmeg
 1 tablespoon water
 1 teaspoon cornstarch
⅓ cup natural wheat and barley cereal
 2 tablespoons chopped toasted almonds
 2 cups vanilla fat-free yogurt

1. Remove stems and pits from cherries; cut into halves (about 2¼ cups). Combine cherries, apple juice, cinnamon and nutmeg in small saucepan; cook and stir over medium heat 5 minutes or until cherries begin to soften.

2. Blend water and cornstarch in small cup until smooth. Stir into saucepan; cook and stir over high heat until mixture boils and thickens slightly. Let cool 10 minutes; cover and refrigerate until chilled.

3. Combine cereal and almonds in small cup. Layer half of cherry mixture, half of yogurt and half of cereal mixture in four 10-ounce wine or parfait glasses; repeat layers.   *Makes 4 servings*

Nutrients per Serving (1 parfait)

Calories: 257, **Total Fat:** 5g, **Saturated Fat:** 1g, **Cholesterol:** 7mg, **Sodium:** 140mg, **Carbohydrate:** 46g, **Fiber:** 3g, **Protein:** 9g

banana coffee cake

½ cup 100% bran cereal
½ cup strong brewed coffee
1 cup mashed ripe bananas (about 2 bananas)
½ cup sugar
1 egg, lightly beaten
2 tablespoons canola or vegetable oil
½ cup all-purpose flour
½ cup whole wheat flour
2 teaspoons baking powder
1 teaspoon ground cinnamon
¼ teaspoon salt

1. Preheat oven to 350°F. Spray 8-inch square baking dish with nonstick cooking spray.

2. Combine cereal and coffee in large bowl; let stand 3 minutes or until cereal softens. Stir in bananas, sugar, egg and oil.

3. Combine all-purpose flour, whole wheat flour, baking powder, cinnamon and salt in small bowl; stir into banana mixture just until moistened. Pour batter into prepared pan.

4. Bake 25 to 35 minutes or until toothpick inserted into center comes out clean. Cool in pan on wire rack. Cut into 9 squares. *Makes 9 servings*

Nutrients per Serving (1 piece)

Calories: 169, **Total Fat:** 4g, **Saturated Fat:** <1g, **Cholesterol:** 24mg, **Sodium:** 166mg, **Carbohydrate:** 30g, **Fiber:** 3g, **Protein:** 3g

Banana Coffee Cake

three-fruit crumble

1 large sweet apple (such as Jonagold or Gala), peeled, cored and cut into 1-inch pieces

1 large ripe pear, peeled, cored and cut into 1-inch pieces

½ cup fresh cranberries

2 tablespoons apricot fruit spread

1 tablespoon sucralose-based sugar substitute or granulated sugar

½ teaspoon cinnamon, divided

⅛ teaspoon salt

⅛ teaspoon ground ginger

1 tablespoon water

1 teaspoon all-purpose flour

¼ cup old-fashioned oats

½ cup high-fiber cereal with small clusters

2 teaspoons packed brown sugar

1 tablespoon margarine, cut in small pieces

⅓ cup plain fat-free Greek-style yogurt

1½ teaspoons granulated sugar

⅛ teaspoon vanilla extract

1. Preheat oven to 350°F. Spray 8-inch square baking dish with nonstick cooking spray.

2. Combine apple, pear, cranberries, fruit spread, sugar substitute, ¼ teaspoon cinnamon, salt and ginger in large bowl. Blend water and flour in cup. Add to fruit mixture; mix well. Spoon fruit mixture into prepared baking dish.

3. Combine oats, cereal, remaining ¼ teaspoon cinnamon and brown sugar in medium bowl. Add margarine; mix with fingertips or fork to form coarse crumbs. Sprinkle over fruit.

4. Bake 40 to 45 minutes or until fruit is tender and bubbly and topping is browned.

5. Combine yogurt, granulated sugar and vanilla in small bowl until well blended. Spoon crumble into four bowls; top each serving with dollop of yogurt mixture.

Makes 4 servings

Nutrients per Serving (⅔ cup crumble with about 4 teaspoons yogurt mixture)

Calories: 169, **Total Fat:** 4g, **Saturated Fat:** 1g, **Cholesterol:** <1mg, **Sodium:** 158mg, **Carbohydrate:** 34g, **Fiber:** 4g, **Protein:** 3g

frozen chocolate-covered bananas

2 ripe medium bananas
4 wooden craft sticks
½ cup low-fat granola cereal without raisins
⅓ cup hot fudge topping, at room temperature

1. Line baking sheet with waxed paper.

2. Peel bananas; cut in half crosswise. Insert wooden stick about 1½ inches into center of cut end of each banana half. Place on prepared baking sheet; freeze at least 2 hours or until firm.

3. Place granola in large resealable food storage bag; crush slightly using rolling pin or meat mallet. Transfer granola to shallow plate. Place hot fudge topping in shallow dish.

4. Working with one banana at a time, place frozen banana in hot fudge topping; turn and spread evenly over banana. Immediately place banana on plate with granola; turn to coat. Return coated banana to baking sheet. Repeat with remaining bananas.

5. Freeze at least 2 hours or until hot fudge topping is very firm. Let stand 5 minutes before serving. *Makes 4 servings*

Nutrients per Serving (½ banana)

Calories: 191, **Total Fat:** 4g, **Saturated Fat:** 2g, **Cholesterol:** 3mg, **Sodium:** 132mg, **Carbohydrate:** 38g, **Fiber:** 3g, **Protein:** 3g

mixed berry crisp

1½ cups fresh raspberries

1 cup fresh blackberries

1 cup fresh blueberries

1 tablespoon fresh lemon juice

3 tablespoons frozen pineapple juice concentrate, divided

5 tablespoons all-purpose flour, divided

¾ cup old-fashioned oats

¼ cup walnuts, finely chopped

3 tablespoons packed brown sugar

½ teaspoon ground cinnamon

2 tablespoons melted butter or margarine

1. Preheat oven to 375°F. Spray 8-inch square baking dish with nonstick cooking spray.

2. Combine berries, lemon juice and 2 tablespoons juice concentrate in medium bowl. Sprinkle with 2 tablespoons flour; toss gently. Spoon into prepared baking dish.

3. Combine oats, walnuts, brown sugar, cinnamon, remaining 3 tablespoons flour and 1 tablespoon juice concentrate in small bowl. Pour butter over oat mixture; mix well. Sprinkle over fruit mixture.

4. Bake about 30 minutes or until fruit is hot and topping is golden brown. Serve warm. *Makes 6 servings*

Nutrients per Serving (½ cup)

Calories: 212, **Total Fat:** 9g, **Saturated Fat:** 2g, **Cholesterol:** 11mg, **Sodium:** 33mg, **Carbohydrate:** 33g, **Fiber:** 5g, **Protein:** 4g

Mixed Berry Crisp

bananas foster sundaes

2 tablespoons packed brown sugar

2 teaspoons butter

1 tablespoon water

1 medium banana, peeled and cut into ¼-inch slices

1 teaspoon rum extract

2 cups vanilla sugar-free reduced-fat ice cream

  Wafer cookie pieces (optional)

1. Heat brown sugar and butter in medium nonstick skillet over medium-low heat, stirring constantly. Add water; cook and stir 30 to 45 seconds or until slightly thickened. Add banana and rum extract, stirring gently to coat banana slices with caramel. Cook about 30 seconds or until heated through.

2. Scoop ice cream into four individual dessert dishes; spoon banana mixture over ice cream. Garnish with cookie pieces. Serve immediately.   *Makes 4 servings*

Nutrients per Serving (½ cup ice cream with 2 tablespoons topping)

Calories: 172, **Total Fat:** 4g, **Saturated Fat:** 2g, **Cholesterol:** 15mg, **Sodium:** 71mg, **Carbohydrate:** 30g, **Fiber:** 2g, **Protein:** 3g

berries with banana cream

½ small ripe banana, cut into chunks

⅓ cup reduced-fat sour cream

1 tablespoon frozen orange juice concentrate

2 cups sliced strawberries, blueberries, raspberries or a combination

⅛ teaspoon ground cinnamon or nutmeg

1. Combine banana, sour cream and juice concentrate in blender; blend until smooth.

2. Divide berries between two serving dishes. Top with sour cream mixture; sprinkle with cinnamon.   *Makes 2 servings*

Nutrients per Serving (1 cup berries with about 3 tablespoons sour cream mixture)

Calories: 162, **Total Fat:** 6g, **Saturated Fat:** 3g, **Cholesterol:** 20mg, **Sodium:** 26mg, **Carbohydrate:** 27g, **Fiber:** 6g, **Protein:** 3g

whole grain cranberry chocolate chip cookies

1½ cups uncooked five-grain cereal

1 cup whole wheat flour

½ teaspoon salt

½ teaspoon baking soda

¼ teaspoon baking powder

½ cup (1 stick) unsalted butter, softened

⅓ cup packed light brown sugar

1 egg

½ teaspoon vanilla

½ cup golden raisins

½ cup semisweet chocolate chips

½ cup sweetened dried cranberries, chopped

1. Preheat oven to 350°F. Spray nonstick cookie sheet with nonstick cooking spray. Combine cereal, flour, salt, baking soda and baking powder in medium bowl.

2. Beat butter and brown sugar in large bowl with electric mixer until light and fluffy. Beat in egg and vanilla until well combined. Beat in flour mixture just until blended. Fold in raisins, chocolate chips and cranberries. Drop dough by tablespoonfuls 2 inches apart on prepared cookie sheet.

3. Bake in center of oven 7 to 9 minutes or until golden. Remove cookies to wire rack to cool completely.   *Makes about 18 cookies*

Variations: Substitute other multigrain cooked cereals for the five-grain cereal. Substitute chopped dried apricots or cherries for the dried cranberries.

Nutrients per Serving (1 cookie)

Calories: 182, **Total Fat:** 8g, **Saturated Fat:** 4g, **Cholesterol:** 25mg, **Sodium:** 114mg, **Carbohydrate:** 28g, **Fiber:** 4g, **Protein:** 3g

fruit kabobs with raspberry yogurt dip

½ cup plain fat-free yogurt

¼ cup no-sugar-added raspberry fruit spread

1 pint fresh strawberries

2 cups cubed honeydew melon (1-inch cubes)

2 cups cubed cantaloupe (1-inch cubes)

1 can (8 ounces) pineapple chunks in juice, drained

Combine yogurt and fruit spread in small bowl until well blended. Thread fruit onto six 12-inch wooden skewers; serve with dip. *Makes 6 servings*

Nutrients per Serving (1 kabob with 2 tablespoons dip)

Calories: 108, **Total Fat:** <1g, **Saturated Fat:** <1g, **Cholesterol:** <1mg, **Sodium:** 52mg, **Carbohydrate:** 25g, **Fiber:** 2g, **Protein:** 2g

pomegranate-glazed pears

4 firm Bosc pears

1 cup pomegranate, blueberry or cranberry-cherry juice

1 to 2 tablespoons honey, or to taste

¼ teaspoon ground cinnamon

½ cup crushed biscotti

1. Peel pears; cut lengthwise into quarters. Remove and discard cores and stem. Place pears in large skillet.

2. Whisk juice, honey and cinnamon in small bowl until well blended. Pour over pears; bring to a boil over medium-high heat. Reduce heat to low; simmer about 10 minutes or until pears are tender, turning occasionally.

3. Remove pears to serving plates with slotted spoon; keep warm. Boil liquid 3 to 4 minutes or until reduced and syrupy. Drizzle glaze over pears; sprinkle with biscotti. *Makes 4 servings*

Nutrients per Serving

Calories: 156, **Total Fat:** 1g, **Saturated Fat:** 0g, **Cholesterol:** 0mg, **Sodium:** 15mg, **Carbohydrate:** 40g, **Fiber:** 5g, **Protein:** 1g

Fruit Kabobs with Raspberry Yogurt Dip

shortcake cobbler

2 cups pear slices

2 cups frozen peach slices, partially thawed

2 tablespoons raisins

¼ cup water

3 packets sugar substitute

2 teaspoons cornstarch

¼ teaspoon vanilla extract

1 cup reduced-fat biscuit baking mix

½ cup plain fat-free yogurt

2 tablespoons sugar

2 tablespoons reduced-fat margarine, melted

1 teaspoon grated orange peel

¼ teaspoon ground cinnamon

1. Preheat oven to 425°F. Spray 11×7-inch baking dish with nonstick cooking spray.

2. Combine pears, peaches and raisins in prepared dish. Combine water, sugar substitute, cornstarch and vanilla in small bowl; stir until cornstarch dissolves. Pour over fruit; toss gently.

3. Combine baking mix, yogurt, sugar, margarine, orange peel and cinnamon in medium bowl; stir until well blended and mixture forms stiff batter. Spoon batter onto fruit mixture in 8 mounds.

4. Bake 20 minutes or until topping is golden brown. Serve warm or at room temperature.

Makes 8 servings

Nutrients per Serving (½ cup)

Calories: 153, **Total Fat:** 3g, **Saturated Fat:** <1g, **Cholesterol:** <1mg, **Sodium:** 235mg, **Carbohydrate:** 32g, **Fiber:** 3g, **Protein:** 3g

Shortcake Cobbler

VOLUME MEASUREMENTS (dry)

$1/8$ teaspoon = 0.5 mL
$1/4$ teaspoon = 1 mL
$1/2$ teaspoon = 2 mL
$3/4$ teaspoon = 4 mL
1 teaspoon = 5 mL
1 tablespoon = 15 mL
2 tablespoons = 30 mL
$1/4$ cup = 60 mL
$1/3$ cup = 75 mL
$1/2$ cup = 125 mL
$2/3$ cup = 150 mL
$3/4$ cup = 175 mL
1 cup = 250 mL
2 cups = 1 pint = 500 mL
3 cups = 750 mL
4 cups = 1 quart = 1 L

VOLUME MEASUREMENTS (fluid)

1 fluid ounce (2 tablespoons) = 30 mL
4 fluid ounces ($1/2$ cup) = 125 mL
8 fluid ounces (1 cup) = 250 mL
12 fluid ounces ($1 1/2$ cups) = 375 mL
16 fluid ounces (2 cups) = 500 mL

WEIGHTS (mass)

$1/2$ ounce = 15 g
1 ounce = 30 g
3 ounces = 90 g
4 ounces = 120 g
8 ounces = 225 g
10 ounces = 285 g
12 ounces = 360 g
16 ounces = 1 pound = 450 g

DIMENSIONS

$1/16$ inch = 2 mm
$1/8$ inch = 3 mm
$1/4$ inch = 6 mm
$1/2$ inch = 1.5 cm
$3/4$ inch = 2 cm
1 inch = 2.5 cm

OVEN TEMPERATURES

250°F = 120°C
275°F = 140°C
300°F = 150°C
325°F = 160°C
350°F = 180°C
375°F = 190°C
400°F = 200°C
425°F = 220°C
450°F = 230°C

BAKING PAN SIZES

Utensil	Size in Inches/Quarts	Metric Volume	Size in Centimeters
Baking or Cake Pan (square or rectangular)	8×8×2	2 L	20×20×5
	9×9×2	2.5 L	23×23×5
	12×8×2	3 L	30×20×5
	13×9×2	3.5 L	33×23×5
Loaf Pan	8×4×3	1.5 L	20×10×7
	9×5×3	2 L	23×13×7
Round Layer Cake Pan	8×1½	1.2 L	20×4
	9×1½	1.5 L	23×4
Pie Plate	8×1¼	750 mL	20×3
	9×1¼	1 L	23×3
Baking Dish or Casserole	1 quart	1 L	—
	1½ quart	1.5 L	—
	2 quart	2 L	—